W9-DFM-975

A GUIDE TO TRACING YOUR DONEGAL ANCESTORS

A guide to tracing your Donegal Ancestors

Godfrey F. Duffy

First published 1995 by
Flyleaf Press
4 Spencer Villas
Glenageary
Co Dublin
Ireland
Ph (01) 2806228

© 1996 Flyleaf Press

British Library cataloguing in Publication Data available

ISBN 0 9508466 6 X

Cover design by Cathy Henderson

Printed by Colour Books, Dublin

Dedication

To my late father Frank whose pride in
his Donegal roots was an inspiration to me.

'Donegal is where I was born,
Later to learn it was in the harvest time,
The briar rich with blackberry,
The fields were full of golden corn.'

From 'Memories' by my Father-in-Law
Hugh Friel, native of Dunfanaghy

Acknowledgements

In researching material for this book a number of people provided assistance for which I am grateful: Joan Patton of Donegal Ancestry for particular information concerning parish registers; Greg O'Connor of the NAI for acquainting me with the most recently acquired archive material. Liam O'Rónáin of Donegal County Library and Pat O'Dougherty of O'Dochartaigh Clan Research at Inch Island; The staff of the PRONI, NLI and other institutions. I am most grateful to Dr. James G. Ryan who initially encouraged me to write the book and whose editorial and genealogical knowledge was invaluable.

Table of Contents

Abbreviations

Bapts	Baptisms
BL	British Library
Co.	County
CDB	Congested Districts Board
Chap.	Chapter
DAL	Donegal Ancestry Ltd
DKPRONI	(Reports of the) Deputy Keeper of Public Records Office (NI)
DKPROI	(Reports of the) Deputy Keeper of Public Records Office
Don. Ann.	Donegal Annual
GO	Genealogical Office
GRO	General Register Office
HLD	Genealogical Centre, Heritage Library, Derry
IGI	International Genealogical Index
IGRS	Irish Genealogical Research Society
ILC	Irish Land Commission
IMC	Irish Manuscripts Commission
JAPMD	Journal of the Association for the Preservation of the Memorials of the Dead (in Ireland)
LC	Local Custody. (Most churches hold their original registers.)
LDS	Church of Jesus-Christ of Latter-Day Saints
mf	Microfilm
m/fiche	Microfiche
Ms	Manuscript
NAI	National Archives of Ireland (Formerly the PRO)
NLI	National Library of Ireland

P	Positive (mf)
PLU	Poor Law Union
PRO	Public Record Office, Dublin (now National Archives)
PRONI	Public Record Office Northern Ireland
Pub.	Published
RCBL	Representative Church Body Library
Ref	Reference
SLC	Salt Lake City Geneological Library (LDS HQ)
T	Transcript

Chapter 1 Introduction

According to Celtic mythology the Milesians (Ibero-Celts) settled in the area that is now Co. Donegal and one of the first recognised kings of Ulster, 'Niall Naoigiallach' (Niall of the Nine Hostages), claimed descent from them. Niall with his sons, Eoghan and Conall carved out a powerful, independent kingdom in the 5th century AD. Indeed Tir Conall 'Conall's land' was the ancient name for Donegal. Donegal from the Irish Dún na nGall 'fort of the foreigner' was the later name.

Conall and Eoghan's descendants became the great clans of O'Donnell and O'Neill. The clans themselves consisted of many families bound together through blood and loyalty.

There have always been close links between Donegal and Scotland. In the medieval period Scots mercenaries known as 'gallowglasses' arrived to do service in the armies of O'Donnell and O'Neill.

Many people today with Donegal ancestry will be descended from the O'Neill, O'Donnell and gallowglasses clans.

After a thousand years Gaelic power was finally broken by English expansionism. During the 17th century the land of Gaelic chieftains was confiscated by the victors, namely English Protestants who became the new landlords. English Protestants and Scots Presbyterians were offered land to secure loyal tenantry. This policy was actively pursued by the English administration and was known as the Plantation. It affected Donegal and its records. From this period English and Scottish surnames appeared in the records to a degree that is disproportionate to their minority status.

The origin of the family name can be significant when researching Donegal ancestors as it may be a clue as to which records to search.

Emigration from the 18th to the 20th century saw Donegal people of all religions and backgrounds leaving for Britain, America and further afield.

Dress. the blind, and to such persons as were residents in the parish. The holyday-dress of the people here is neat, and sometimes borders on finery; whereas their every day dress assimilates to their mode of living.

Small-Pox. A few children have fallen victims to the confluent small-pox this year, which is the only distemper that affects the population of this parish : to counteract which, I have inoculated the children of those poor, near myself, who applied to me for the purpose, with vaccine infection ; but I regret to say, that the people here, with a few exceptions, are prejudiced against it, thinking that the vaccine system will protect them from the ravages of the small-pox only three years. It is a subject, I think, that requires parliamentary consideration.

VI. *The Genius & Disposition of the Poorer Classes, &c.*

Genius. The genius of the people turns on an agricultural axis, although there are some expert craftsmen in the parish, such as, shoemakers, weavers, carpenters, coopers, wheelwrights, &c. : they are remarkably sober, regular, and attentive to business; spirited, warlike, and courageous, yet not by any means quarrelsome; they are charitable to the poor, and a kind good-natured peasantry as ever I knew.

Language. The vernacular language is what is used by the people in common, although they are acquiring a tolerable knowledge of the English now, since their ideas were whetted by a commercial intercourse in the neighbouring fairs and markets. It may be right to remark here, that some of the old men in this parish have a genius for reading the Irish language, in Irish characters, and there is one old man, upwards of 80 years

An account of Donegal people from William Shaw Mason's 'Statistical Account or Parochial Survey of Ireland' 1814.

Records went with these people and new records were started in their adopted countries.

This guide concentrates on Donegal records available in Ireland for the period when the greatest amount of records was generated covering the majority of the population.

MONAGHAN

- - - - - - - - -   Border between Northern Ireland and the Irish Republic

Donegal and Surrounding Counties

Chapter 2   How to Use this Book

The family name(s), and perhaps some oral tradition or documentary evidence, is often the only vestige of our ancestry we possess. However, many people who are justly proud to claim Irish descent will want to investigate more fully their history and origins. By doing so, they can place their family in the context of the history of the country, and see them as real people who lived through, and perhaps significantly contributed to, the great and traumatic periods in our history.

This book sets out to assist those with Donegal origins to learn about their ancestry. It is designed to guide the reader through the many types of documents and sources which record the lives of the people of Donegal.

The bulk of genealogical material relating to Co. Donegal refers to the 19th century. Although sources such as the 1901 and 1911 census list people born in the 19th century (see Chap. 6), Census substitutes eg. the Primary Valuation and Tithe Applottment Books can list people born both in the 19th and 18th centuries (see Chap. 6).

Parish registers provide a rich source of genealogical material and may be the only source with which to locate our Donegal ancestors. The Church Records chapter provides information on the majority of extant parish registers with parish maps for Catholic and Church of Ireland parishes (Chap. 4).

Civil registration of all Irish births, deaths and marriages began in 1864 and lists of Co. Donegal registration areas and records available is given in chapter 7.

National school registers are another useful source for locating ancestors once their parish is ascertained (see Chap. 12). Pension claims are another source for locating ancestors (see Chap. 6).

The Land Records chapter, which includes estate papers, can provide information on our ancestors location from the 19th to 18th century (see Chap. 9). Ancestors who belonged to more specific trade, military or social groups can be located in the census substitutes (see Chap. 6).

By the close of the 19th century our more enterprising ancestors were using the newspapers and commercial directories to advertise their businesses (see Chaps. 10 and 11).

It is always worth consulting wills as a source of genealogical material, although not all our ancestors made wills. This depended on their religion and station in life (see Chap. 8).

Finally Donegal family histories have been written on a professional and amateur basis. Some have been published and others have simply been deposited in various institutions (see Chap. 13).

There are many possible starting points for a family history, but a logical first point of contact with the past is your own family lore. It is worth asking family members about family connections and stories. In this context, elderly family members are generally the most useful, but a relation need not necessarily be old to be knowledgeable.

To organise your family investigation of 'missing' and known family members, a 'Family Tree' chart should be drawn up. It is suggested by family history societies that such charts should at least show up to 30 direct ancestors including your parents. Index cards or a computer family tree data-base can be used to highlight each ancestors' personal details e.g. name/surname, date of birth/baptism, marriage, death/burial, place of birth, residence and occupation.

In attempting a family history, good preparation is important. To this end a few practical guidelines are suggested.

1. It is useful to know the history of Co. Donegal both at local and county level to understand the range of events which may have affected your family, or have resulted in records.

2. Set a goal for your research, eg tracing a specific line of descent, or finding a specific ancestor, rather than trying to find all lines at the same time.

3. Record all the information you find, including conversations. It is in the nature of genealogy that the significance of material initially examined may not be realised until later.

4. Begin the research with yourself and proceed into the past one generation at a time, i.e. always work from the known to the unknown.

Chapter 3   Administrative Divisions.

Most of the records useful in family research are drawn up by some form of local administration, whether of a governmental, religious or other nature. To find family information in these records, it is important to know the areas within which these administrators worked. The following are the land divisions used in Donegal. They are referred to extensively within the book, and a knowledge of them is important.

Province: The four provinces of Ireland, Ulster, Connacht, Munster and Leinster date from at least the 5th century. Co. Donegal is in the province of Ulster as are the counties of Derry, Tyrone, Fermanagh, Armagh, Down, Antrim, Cavan and Monaghan. The term 'Ulster' is used incorrectly in some popular contexts to denote the 6 counties of Ireland which are within the UK. However, Donegal, Cavan and Monaghan are all within the Republic of Ireland.

County: The division of Ireland into counties began in the late 12th century with Dublin and the process gradually continued until the formation of the last county, Wicklow in 1606. Co. Donegal was formed from the Lordship of the O'Donnell clan during the plantation of Ulster in the early 17th century. Co. Donegal is bordered by counties Leitrim, Fermanagh, Tyrone and Derry. (See Map p. 14)

Barony: The barony was used as an administrative division from the 16th century and is featured in the Civil Survey, Down Survey and Books of Survey and Distribution. During the 18th century county rates fixed by the Grand Juries were paid on a barony basis. Once again in the 19th century the barony was used in the Primary Valuation. Its use continued into the 20th century when it was used as an enumeration unit in the 1901 census. The baronies of Co. Donegal are East and West Inishowen, Kilmacrenan, Boylagh, Banagh, Tirhugh and Raphoe North and South.

Civil Parish: This is perhaps the most widely used land division in local records. Note that a parish may encompass several unconnected pieces of land in a single county, and that a parish may straddle a county boundary. In general the Civil parish coincides with the Church of Ireland parish.

Townland: This is the smallest of the administrative divisions, their size varying from 1 to 7,000 acres. In rural areas the townland is the basic 'address' used by the people. Generations of certain families lived within certain townlands to the extent that local people will associate a townland with a particular family. A complete list of the townlands of Ireland and their location (within civil parish, Barony, PLU etc) can be found in the 'General Alphabetical Index to the Townlands and Towns, Parishes and Baronies of Ireland', Thoms 1861.

Poor Law Union: The Poor Law Union Relief Act of 1838 established a tax to be levied on property owners for the welfare of the poor. For this purpose the country was divided into Poor Law Unions (PLU). Each Union had a workhouse   based in a main town and the PLU's were named after these towns. The PLUs of Co. Donegal were Inishowen, Dunfanaghy, Londonderry, Milford, Glenties, Letterkenny, Stranorlar, Donegal and Ballyshannon. (See p. 42)   Each Union was further sub-divided into District Electoral Divisions. See p. 86 for records held by Donegal County Archive.

Superintendent Registrar's Districts: These areas are geographically identical to the Poor Law Unions (see above) and were used as administrative areas in collection of birth, marriage and death records.

Archdiocese: The Synod of Kells in 1152 established the archdioceses of Armagh, Tuam, Cashel and Dublin. The Armagh archdiocese contains the dioceses of Raphoe, Derry and Clogher and parts of each encompass Co. Donegal. Their diocesan centres are at Letterkenny, Derry and Monaghan. Both Raphoe and Clogher have diocesan archives.

After the Reformation the Church of Ireland became the State or established church in Ireland. From this time the Catholic Church and Church of Ireland were independently administered and their dioceses and parish boundaries do not coincide. Church of Ireland parishes are co-extensive with civil parishes (see Map p. 27) while Catholic parishes have separate boundaries.

Ecclesiastical Parishes: Since the Reformation the Roman Catholic Church and Church of Ireland have been separately administered.

The Catholic parishes were usually larger than their Church of Ireland counterparts and were regularly reorganised to accommodate changing demographic situations (see map p. 23) .

The Church of Ireland was the official State Church and had jurisdiction over wills and administrations, and other civil duties. It was also supported by tithes which were paid by the public of all persuasions. Their parishes are coextensive with Civil parishes (see map p. 27)

Chapter 4   Church Records

The 1861 Government Census recorded the denominational membership of Donegal residents as 75% Catholic; 12.6% Protestant; 11% Presbyterian and 1% Methodist. Records of all these churches exist, and are the only record of the existence of many, if not most, of the people of Donegal.

Catholic Church Records

Although Roman Catholicism was the religion of the majority of the Donegal population, various measures were used by the Crown, particularly in the 18th century, to suppress the Catholic church and disadvantage its members. It was only at the close of the 18th century that a relaxation of these 'Penal laws' occurred.

The practical consequence of this for family history is that Catholic Churches were poorer and less well organised. Significant factors determining whether churches kept records included the wealth of the parish, and the competence and inclination of the priests and their bishops. In general the larger towns have the earliest registers and rural registers generally start later. A full description of the factors affecting record keeping is given in Ryan (1992) Irish Church Records. (see p. 85)

In comparison with other Irish counties, Donegal has poor Catholic records. The earliest extant registers are for Clonleigh and Urney, and date from 1773. However, the majority of the remainder date from the mid 19th century. They vary widely in legibility and are written in either Latin or English.

The National Library of Ireland (NLI) microfilmed the majority of Catholic registers in the 1950's and these microfilms are accessible there, as well as in many County Heritage Centres. In the NLI index to microfilms they are organised by diocese, and it is therefore useful to know the Diocese to which each parish of interest belongs. Derry and Raphoe dioceses cover all of Co. Donegal except for two parishes which are in Clogher diocese.

The Catholic parishes of Donegal are listed below, together with a reference to their position on the map (p. 23). The most recent parishes were formed from older parishes in the same geographical area. In these cases the map reference number is the same. The baptism, marriage and burial registers are extant from the date stated and can be found in one or all of the archival centres listed. Those listed here are those which start before 1895.

Co. Donegal: Catholic Parish Registers

Parish	Map Ref.	Bapts.	Marriage	Burials	Location
All Saints, Killea Taughboyne	32	1843	1843		NLI/DAL /HLD
Annagry	26	1868			NLI
Ardara	28	1868	1867		NLI/DAL
Arranmore Island	25	1886	1887		DAL
Aughnish & Aghaninshin	16	1873	1873	1873	NLI/DAL
Ballyfin	28	1890	1894		DAL
Burt	22	1859	1856	1860	NLI/HLD
Carn	50	1851	1836		NLI
Churchill	14	1884	1920		DAL
Clonca	1	1856	1870		NLI/DAL
Clondahorky	10	1877	1879		NLI
Clondavaddog	7	1847	1847	1847	NLI/DAL
Clonleigh	35	1773	1781		NLI/HLD
Clonmany	2	1852	1852		NLI/HLD
Conwal & Leck	30	1853	1853		NLI/DAL
Culdaff	4	1838	1849		NLI/DAL
Desertegney	21	1864	1871		NLI/HLD
Donagh	3	1847	1849		NLI/HLD
Donaghmore	39	1840	1846		NLI
Drumholm	49	1866	1866		NLI/DAL
Drumkeen		1893	1893		DAL
Raymochey	31	1854	1855		DAL
Dunfanaghy	15	1856	1856		DAL
Falcarragh	10	1889	1887		DAL

Parish	Map Ref.	Bapts.	Marriage	Burials	Location
Gartan					
& Termon	14	1862			NLI/DAL
Glencolmcille	42	1879	1881		NLI/DAL
Glenswilly	17	1874	1877		DAL
Glenvar	12	1888	1843		DAL
Gortahork	9	1849	1861		NLI
Gweedore	8	1868	1866		NLI/DAL
Inishkeel	28	1866	1866		NLI/DAL
Innishmacsaint	52	1848	1847		NLI
Inver	46	1861	1861		NLI/DAL
Iskaheen	6	1858			NLI/HLD
Kilbarron	51	1854	1858		NLI/DAL
Kilcar	43	1848			NLI/DAL
Kilclonney	28	1885			DAL
Kilmacrenan	15	1862	1863		NLI/DAL
Killaghtee	45	1845	1857		NLI/DAL
Killybegs	44	1850	1850		NLI/DAL
Killygarvan					
&Tullyfern	12	1868	1873		NLI/DAL
Killymard	47	1874			NLI/DAL
Kincasslagh	25	1877	1878		DAL
Kilteevogue	37	1855	1855		NLI/DAL
Lettermacward &	27	1876	1877		NLI/DAL
Templecrone					
Mevagh	11	1871	1878		NLI/DAL
Milford	12	1874	1885		DAL
Moville Lr	5	1847	1847	1847	NLI/HLD
NewtonCunningham	32	1857			DAL
Raphoe	36	1876	1876		NLI/DAL
Rathmullan	12	1859	1873		DAL
Stranorlar	38	1860	1877		NLI/DAL
Tawnawilly	48	1872	1882		DAL
Tullabegley/	9	1868			NLI
Raymunterdoney,					
Tory Is. &					
Urney	40	1773			NLI

Index to Catholic Parishes on map opposite

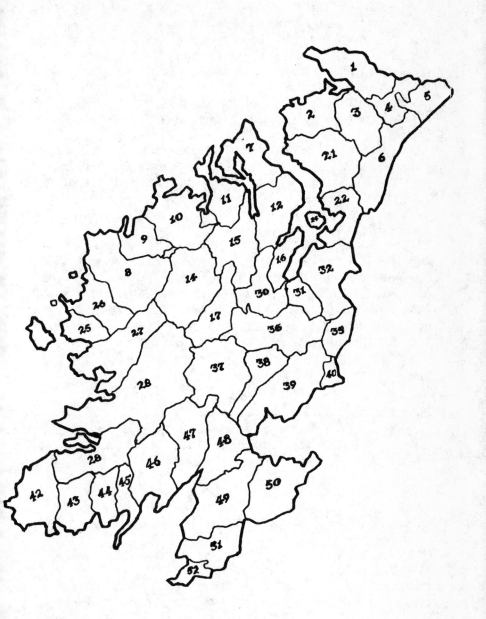

Catholic Parishes of Co. Donegal

Church of Ireland Records

The Church of Ireland (also known as Protestant, Episcopal or Anglican church) was the state or Established church from the 16th century until 1869 and in this capacity had jurisdiction over will probate, marriage and some other functions. Its clergy often held important positions within the community and its churches were at one time the only churches where worship was allowed. Its grave-yards were the resting place not only for Church of Ireland parishioners but also parishioners of other denominations. A full account of the records of the Church of Ireland is given by Refausse (1992) Irish Church Records. (see p. 85)

In 1869 the Church of Ireland ceased to be the state church and under the Public Record Act (1867) the PRO took charge of the Church of Ireland's baptism and burial registers up to 1870 and marriage registers up to 1845. From 1845 the Registrar General had supplied pro forma marriage registers to all Protestant churches to facilitate state registration of marriage. (see Civil Registration p. 43).

When the PRO caught fire in the Civil War of 1922, there were registers from 1006 Church of Ireland parishes in the PRO. Only a few parish registers survived. However 637 parishes had records in local custody and other parishes had copied their registers before sending them to the PRO.

County Donegal has a fairly good collection of Church of Ireland registers in comparison with other counties. The earliest are those of Drumholm from 1691. The majority of registers however date from the 19th century and are all written in English.

Co. Donegal: Church of Ireland Registers

Parish	Map Ref.	Bapts.	Marriage	Burials	Location
All Saints	29	1877	1845	1820	DAL
Ardara		1829	1829	1830	DAL/RCBL/LC
Aughaninshin	18	1878	1845	1878	RCBL
Burt	25	1809	1809	1809	DAL/RCBL/LC
Clonca	1	1669		1783	JAPMD, Vol V, No.3 (1903)
Clondahorky E	10	1871	1845	1884	DAL/RCBL
Clondahorky W	10	1873	1873		DAL
Clondavaddog	7	1794	1794	1794	DAL/LC
Clonleigh	35	1872	1845	1877	RCBL
Convoy	36	1871	1844	1881	DAL/RCBL
Conwal	17	1876	1845	1878	RCBL

Parish	Map Ref.	Bapts.	Marriage	Burials	Location
Craigadooish				1871	RCBL
Culdaff	4	1875	1845	1876	RCBL
Desertegney	20	1790	1813	1803	DAL/RCBL/LC
Donaghmore	39	1818	1817	1825	DAL/RCBL
Donegal	48	1808	1812	1812	DAL/LC
Drumholm	49	1691	1691	1696	DAL/LC
Dunfanaghy		1873	1875	1873	DAL
Dunlewey		1853	1853		RCBL/LC
Fahan Lr	21	1817	1817	1822	DAL/RCBL
Fahan Up.	22	1762	1765	1765	DAL/RCBL/LC
Finner		1815	1815	1815	LC
Gartan	14	1881	1845		RCBL
Glenalla		1871	1871	1906	DAL/RCBL
Glencolmcille	42	1827	1845	1827	DAL/RCBL/LC
Gleneely		1872	1859		RCBL
Glenties		1827	1856RAM	1898	DAL/RCBL/LC
Goland C. of Ease		1847			DAL
Gweedore		1880	1855	1881	DAL/RCBL
Inch	24	1868	1846	1868	DAL/RCBL
Inniskeel	28	1699-1700	1699-1700	1699-1700	NA
		1818	1818	1818	NA/DAL/LC
		1852	1821	1852	DAL/RCBL
Inver	46	1805	1805	1818	DAL/LC
Kilbarron	51	1785	1785	1785	LC
Kilcar	43	1819	1819	1818	DAL/RCBL/LC
Killaghtee	45	1775	1758	1762	DAL/LC
Killea	33	1877	1845	1880	DAL/RCBL
Kilteevogue	37	1818	1845	1825	RCBL/LC
Killybegs	41+44	1787	1809	1806	DAL/RCBL/LC
Killygarvan	13	1706	1706	1706	DAL
Killymard	47	1880	1845	1819	DAL
Laghey		1877	1847	1877	DAL
Lettermacward	27	1889	1846	1890	DAL/RCBL
Leck	30	1878	1846	1878	RCBL
Lough Eske		1876			DAL
Meenglass			1864		RCBL
Mevagh	11	1876	1846	1877	DAL
Milford		1879	1860		DAL/RCBL
Monellan		1872	1874	1885	DAL

1	Clonca		29	All Saints
2	Clonmany		18	Aughaninshin
3	Donagh		16	Aughnish (2 Parts)
4	Culdaff (2 Parts)		25	Burt
5	Moville Lower (2 Parts)		1	Clonca
6	Moville Upper		10	Clondahorky
7	Clondavaddog		7	Clondavaddog
8	Tullaghobegly		35	Clonleigh
9	Raymunterdoney (4 Parts)		2	Clonmany
10	Clondahorky		36	Convoy
11	Mevagh		17	Conwal
12	Tullyfern		4	Culdaff (2 Parts)
13	Killygarvan		20	Desertegney
14	Gartan		3	Donagh
15	Kilmacrenan (3 Parts)		39	Donaghmore
16	Aughnish (2 Parts)		48	Donegal
17	Conwal		49	Drumholm
18	Aughaninshin		21	Fahan Lower
19	Mintiaghs or Barr of Inch		22	Fahan Upper
20	Desertegney		14	Gartan
21	Fahan Lower		42	Glencolmcille
22	Fahan Up		24	Inch
23	Muff		52	Inishmacsaint
24	Inch		28	Inniskeel
25	Burt		46	Inver
26	Templecrone		51	Kilbarron
27	Lettermacward		43	Kilcar
28	Inniskeel		45	Killaghtee (2 Parts)
29	All Saints		33	Killea
30	Leck (2 Parts)		41	Killybegs Lower (2 Parts)
31	Raymouchy		44	Killybegs Upper
32	Taughboyne		13	Killygarvan
33	Killea		47	Killymard (2 Parts)
34	Raphoe		15	Kilmacrenan (3 Parts)
35	Clonleigh		37	Kilteevogue
36	Convoy		30	Leck (2 Parts)
37	Kilteevogue		27	Lettermacward
38	Stranorlar		11	Mevagh
39	Donaghmore		19	Mintiaghs or Barr of Inch
40	Urney		5	Moville Lr. (2 Parts)
41	Killybegs Lower (2 Parts)		6	Moville Upr.
42	Glencolmcille		23	Muff
43	Kilcar		34	Raphoe
44	Killybegs Upper		31	Raymouchy
45	Killaghtee (2 Parts)		9	Raymunterdoney (4 Parts)
46	Inver		38	Stranorlar
47	Killymard (2 Parts)		32	Taughboyne
48	Donegal		50	Templecarn
49	Drumholm		26	Templecrone
50	Templecarn		8	Tullaghobegly
51	Kilbarron		12	Tullyfern
52	Inishmacsaint		40	Urney

Civil Parishes of Donegal – Map Index

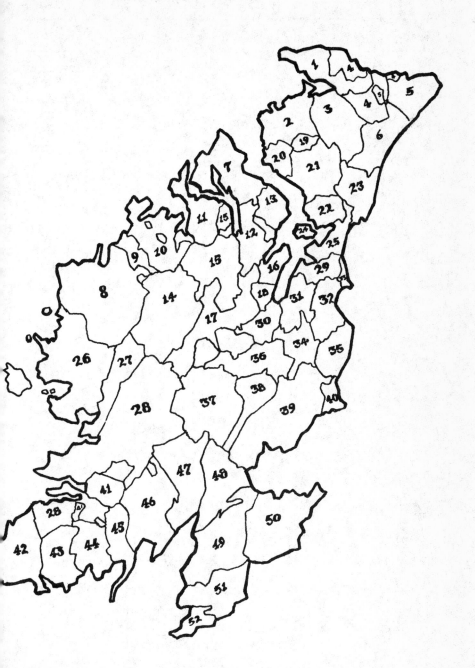

Civil Parish Map of Donegal

Parish	Map Ref.	Bapts.	Marriage	Burials	Location
MountCharles		1877	1861	1860	DAL
Muff	23	1803	1804	1847	RCBL/LC
Newtown Cunningham		1877	1845	1820	RCBL
Raphoe	34	1771	1771	1771	DAL
Raymouchy	31	1844	1845	1878	RCBL
Raymunterdoney	9	1878	1845	1880	DAL
Rossnowlagh		1879	1845		DAL
Stranorlar	38	1802	1821	1821	DAL/RCBL/LC
Taughboyne	32	1820	1820	1820	RCBL/LC
Templecarn	50	1825	1825	1825	RCBL/LC
Templecrone	26	1878	1849	1851	RCBL/DAL/LC
Tullaghobegley	8	1821	1821	1850	DAL/LC
Tullaughnish		1798	1788	1788	DAL/RCBL/LC

The Presbyterian Church

In the 1861 census there were 174,000 Presbyterians in Co. Donegal (11% of the population). This Church was established in Ireland at the start of the 17th century by Scottish Presbyterians, the so-called 'Scots-Irish', and was further encouraged by plantation landlords such as Sir Arthur Chichester in Co. Donegal. The church was mainly based in Ulster. At the end of the 19th century 96% of all Presbyterians lived in Ulster, mainly in the counties of Antrim and Down. Many Presbyterians had also emigrated to pre-revolutionary America and played an active role in the American struggle for independence. A full account of the history of the Presbyterian church, and the types and accessibility of their records is given by Kineally in Irish Church Records (1992). (see p. 85)

There were a number of schisms within the Presbyterian Church in Scotland which also affected the Irish church. In the 19th century a dissenter group known as the Reformed Presbyterians or Covenanters was established and this resulted in more than one Presbyterian church in the same locality. To distinguish these groups, the churches were referred to as 1st and 2nd etc.

Co. Donegal: Presbyterian Parish Registers

Parish	Bapts.	Marriage	Burials	Location
Ballindrait	1819	1845		DAL/PRONI
Ballylennon 1st	1829	1831	1830	DAL/PRONI
Ballylennon 2nd	1845	1845		DAL/PRONI
Ballylennon 3rd	1878			DAL
Ballyshannon	1836	1837		PRONI
Buncrana	1836	1845		PRONI
Burt	1833	1837		DAL/PRONI
Carndonagh	1830	1830		DAL/PRONI
Carnone	1834	1846		PRONI
Carrigart	1844	1844		DAL/PRONI
Convoy	1822	1846		DAL/PRONI
Crossroads	1811	1811		DAL/PRONI
Donegal 1st	1824	1824	1860	DAL/PRONI
Donegal 2nd	1865	1845		DAL/PRONI
Donaghmore	1835	1820	1825	DAL/PRONI
Donaghmore	1834	1846		DAL/PRONI
Drumholm			1845	DAL
Dunfanaghy	1830	1830		DAL/PRONI
Fahan	1899	1845		PRONI

Parish	Bapts.	Marriage	Burials	Location
Fannad	1827	1827		DAL
Fannet	1859	1827		PRONI
Gortlee (Reformed)	1872	1872		DAL/PRONI
Greenbank	1862	1864		DAL
Inch		1845		PRONI
Killymarde		1845		
Kilmacrenan	1848	1846		DAL/PRONI
Knowhead	1826	1846		PRONI
Letterkenny 1st	1845	1845	1845	DAL/PRONI
Letterkenny 2nd	1821	1821		DAL/PRONI
Letterkenny 3rd	1841	1845		DAL/PRONI
Malin	1845	1845		DAL/PRONI
Milford	1838	1845		DAL/PRONI
Milford (Reformed)	1864	1864		DAL
Monreagh	1845	1860		DAL/PRONI
Moville	1833	1845		DAL/PRONI
New Moville	1865			DAL
Newtown Cunningham	1830	1830	1880	PRONI
NW Donegal Mission	1864			DAL
Pettigo	1844	1846		PRONI
Ramelton 1st	1806	1807		DAL/PRONI
Ramelton 2nd	1808	1808		DAL/PRONI
Ramelton 3rd	1839	1839		DAL/PRONI
Raphoe 1st	1829	1829		DAL
Raphoe 2nd	1860	1860		PRONI
Rathmullan	1854	1845		DAL/PRONI
Ray 1st	1855	1845		PRONI
Ray 2nd	1882	1845		PRONI
St. Johnston	1838	1835		DAL/PRONI
Stranorlar	1821	1846	1831	DAL/PRONI
Trentagh	1836	1830	1843	DAL/PRONI
Urney	1837	1866		DAL

The Methodist Church

John Wesley is credited with founding Methodism and he first came to Ireland in 1747. Methodists existed as a group within the established church until about 1878. Some of the earliest Methodist Circuits had been formed in the north of Ireland after 1818. In 1863 Methodists were first allowed to perform marriage ceremonies in their churches. A full account of the range of Methodist church records, and the types and accessibility of their records is in Irish Church Records by Kelly. (see p. 85)

Co. Donegal: Methodist Parish Registers

Parish	Bapts.	Marriage	Burials	Location
Ardara & Dunkineely	1863	1863		DAL
Ballintra	1835			DAL
Donegal Mission	1833	1864		DAL
Inishowen	1862	1873		DAL
Ramelton	1829			DAL

75.—MARY FROM DUNGLOE

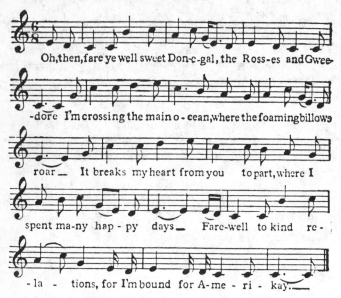

Oh,then,fare ye well sweet Don-e-gal, the Ross-es and Gwee-dore I'm crossing the main o-cean, where the foaming billows roar— It breaks my heart from you to part, where I spent ma-ny hap-py days— Fare-well to kind re-la-tions, for I'm bound for A-me-ri-kay.—

Oh, my love is tall and handsome and her age is scarce eighteen
She far exceeds all other fair maids when she trips over the
    green
Her lovely neck and shoulders are fairer than the snow
Till the day I die I'll ne'er deny my Mary from Dungloe.

If I was at home in Sweet Dungloe a letter I would write
Kind thoughts would fill my bosom for Mary my delight
'Tis in her father's garden, the fairest violets grow
And 'twas there I came to court the maid, my Mary from
    Dungloe.

Ah then, Mary you're my heart's delight my pride and only care
It was your cruel father, would not let me stray there.

148

A popular Donegal Emigrant's song
from Irish Street Ballads, O'Lochlainn, Dublin 1946.

Chapter 5   Gravestone Inscriptions

Gravestone inscriptions are a very useful source of information on dates of birth and death, and also on family relationships. In rural areas it was common practice for generations of the same family to be buried in the same part of the graveyard, and thus information on several generations can be derived from the gravestones where they exist. In poorer areas these were often unmarked graves, although gravestones were sometimes erected by later generations. Fortuitously some gravestones may note previous generations but this is not always the case.

Catholics were sometimes buried in Church of Ireland graveyards and a record could exist in the burial register. Specific Catholic graveyards were started mainly in the 19th century although the local church may not have burial registers until the 20th century. An account of the complicated history of denominational graveyards is given in Irish Church Records (Ryan 1992). (see p. 85)

Some graveyards may be found in apparently isolated locations, since many were attached to ancient monastic sites. Alternatively the attached church may have been abandoned or fallen into ruin. If the present parish church gravestones appear fairly recent it is worth asking local people if an older graveyard exists in the parish.

Gravestones in some graveyards may have already been transcribed or indexed and thus a lot of time and effort can be saved which would have been expended visiting the graveyards in person. However, the majority of graveyards have not. The transcribed gravestones are available in a variety of sources, particularly local history journals. However, there is one major collection which is always worth consulting. This is the Journal of the Association for the Preservation of the Memorials of the Dead

These journals were published in the period 1888-1934 and contain gravestone inscriptions and other information. These were mainly contributed by individuals, and vary from single interesting inscriptions to full graveyard surveys, and occasionally abstracts of other church records. They tended to cover Church of Ireland graveyards, however other denominations could also be buried in these graveyards and may also be recorded. The Journal is indexed by name in various series.

Donegal graveyards partly or wholly abstracted in the Journal of the Association for the Preservation of the Memorials of the Dead

Graveyard	Volume	Number	Year
Ballyshannon (Kilbarron church)	I	1	1890
Kilbarron, Donaghmore	I	1	1891
Fenner (Bundoran), Raymochy	I	1	1891
Raphoe			
Clonca, Mail, Lagg, Moville	IV	1	1898
Glencolmcille, Kilmacrenan			
Clonmany	V	1	1901
Ardmore, Cooly	V	2	1902
Clondohorky	V	3	1903
Carndonagh	VI	1	1904
Gartan	VI	2	1905
Cockhill, Drumnasillagh	VI	3	1906
Old Leck			

Co. Donegal Graveyards Transcribed in other sources

Graveyard	Source
Aghanunshin	DAL*
Assaroe Abbey (Ballyshannon)	DON ANN 1957
Balleeghan	DAL
Ballyshannon, St. Anne's	DAL, DON ANN 1978
Bruckless	DAL
Clonmany (C of Ireland)	Dun Laoghaire Genealogical Journal (Summer 1993)
SS Conal & Joseph	IGRS (GO)
Finner	In 'Where Erne and Drowes Meet the Sea' by Rev. P.O.O'Gallachair, 1961.
Gartan	DAL
Inver	DAL, IGRS (GO)
Inver Old	DAL
Killaghtee	DAL, IGRS (GO)
Killaghtee Old	DAL
Killybegs	DAL, IGRS (GO)
Killydonnell	DAL
Kilmacrenan	DAL
Kilmonaster (Cloneigh)	DAL

Co. Donegal Graveyards Transcribed in other sources cont.

Graveyard	Source
Magheragallon	Irish Family History Vol. V, 1989
Pettigo, Carne	DAL, Don ANN 1989
Raymochy	DAL
Tullaghbegley	DAL
Tullyaughnish	DAL

MAGHERAGALLON OLD GRAVEYARD

Name & Family	Date of Death	Age
Daniel FRIEL, Brinlack	11 August 1929	98 years
his wife Sophia	24 March 1932	92 years
Brid Nic AOIDH, Carrick	17 March 1934	56 years
son Padraig	17 March 1921	3 years
Eoin O BAOILL	8 January 1921	80 years
Mairead Ni BHAOILL	13 August 1911	80 years
Cormack McGEE, Lunniagh	5 September 1869	57 years
his wife Susan	1 August 1912	93 years
Owen GILLESPIE	26 August 1912	74 years
Stranacorkra.		
Sheila COLL	19 January 1915	38 years
Joe GILLESPIE	24 November 1912	3 years
Hannah GILLESPIE	Died in infancy.	
Mary GILLESPIE	11 November 1927	81 years
wife of Owen		
Anne Jane McMANUS nee MacSWEENEY		
Philadelphia	22 July 1929	66 years
her father Turlough	13 June 1916	98 years
her mother Sarah CROSBY	29 November 1920	82 years
Peter GALLAGHER	April 1947	84 years
Strancacorkra.		
his wife Bridget	November 1911	44 years
daughter Bridget	November 1911	18 years
son Dominick	May 1941	38 years
Bridget COYLE	7 June 1898	54 years
Maurice COLL, Inismann	4 August 1912	30 years
Tom COLL	7 September 1912	25 years
Manus COLL	October 1927	42 years

#94#

Abstracts of graveyard inscriptions in Magheragallon Old Graveyard from
Irish Family History Vol. V, 1989

Chapter 6   Censuses and Census Substitutes

Government censuses were compiled every 10 years from 1821. Although the statistics and other analyses of these censuses are available, the only complete surviving census returns are for 1901 and 1911. Some earlier census returns survive for parts of other counties but none survive for County Donegal. The census returns for 1821, 1831, 1841 and 1851 were destroyed in 1922 when the Public Record Office was burnt. Previous to 1922 the British government had officially destroyed the 1861, 1871, 1881, and 1891 census returns for various reasons.

It should be noted that family information had been extracted from the 1841 and 1851 census returns on behalf of pension claimants in the 1908-1921 period and this material is still available. Most Irish people 70 years and over become eligible to claim a pension under the Pension Act (1908) introduced by the British government. Claimants had to provide evidence of their age. Many could produce baptismal details. When these were not available, it was possible to request a search of the 1841 or/and 1851 Census Returns. To do so, the claimant supplied details of their 1841 or 1851 address and family. These claim forms and the results of the searches survive. The searcher, as well as noting the claimant's age in 1841 or/and 1851, often noted the same details for other members of the claimant's family. Both the National Archives and PRONI hold claimant details for Co. Donegal and the PRONI records (T. 550, Vol. 37) cover the parishes of the Inishowen barony in detail.

Apart from official government censuses, there is also a substantial amount of material not originally compiled for an official census, but which provides much the same type of information. These sources list all or selected individuals in a certain area. They were compiled by various religious, political, military and civil groups for a variety of reasons. Such 'census substitutes' continue to come to light.

A selection of Censuses & Census Substitutes for Co. Donegal is as follows:

1612-1613: Undertakers:

> Lists of English and Scottish landlords granted land (Hist. Mss. Comm. Rep. 4 - Hasting Mss) NAI.

1630: Muster Rolls:

Lists of major landlords and able-bodied men at arms (16-60 years) they could muster. The surnames are reflective of the planter ethnic population of English and Scots in Co. Donegal, NLI m/f P. 206; Don Ann 10 (2)(1972) 124-149; Co. Don. Lib. (see p. 63)

1640-1688: Books of Survey and Distribution:

Books show changes in land ownership that had taken place since 1640. The distribution shows changes of ownership before and after the confiscations of the 1650's and the Act of Settlement and Explanations of the 1660's plus the forfeitures of 1688. Books are divided by county and parish.

1642: Muster Roll:

SLC m/f 897012

1654: Civil Survey:

Records of land ownership compiled 1654-1656 and more detailed than the Books of Survey & Distribution. The Civil Survey contains topographical and descriptive features, wills, deeds. (IMC publication, Vol III, I 6551) and Co. Don.. Lib.

1659: Census of Ireland:

Lists of 'tituladoes' i.e. people entitled to land. Divided into respective baronies, parishes and townlands. Lists of number of Irish, Scots and English in each townland; the principal surnames and their frequency is also noted.

1665: Hearth Money Rolls:

Lists those liable to pay a tax based on the number of hearths per house. Listed by head of household in their respective barony, parish and townland. NLI. ms 958314; PRONI. T. 307A. (Listed in 'Laggan and its Presbyterianism' Leck. 1905.)

1718: William Connolly's Ballyshannon Estate.

William Connolly's Ballyshannon Estate. Don. Ann. 33(1981) 27–44. Tenants and their holdings in 1718 & 1726.

1726: See Connolly Estate 1718

[18]

	Wheels.			Wheels.
James Craig	2	John Ward		2
James M'Michael	2	James Ward		2
John Dogherty	2	William Hills		2
William Herald	1	John Ward		2
Alexander Craig	1	James Dolan		2
Thomas Diermot	1	Michael Cunningham		2
William Templeton	1	John Gallaugher		2
James M'Garvey	1	John Mondy		2
James Dogherty	1	Bryan Roper		2
Michael Dermot	1	Matthew Mulherrin		2
		George Sweeney		2

Prsh. of KILLIBEGS.

	Wheels.			
Thomas M'Grath	2	James Sheerin		2
Robert Grunlaw	1	Michael Quin		2
Albert M'Ilwain	1	Barnaby Elliot		2
Charles Blean	1	Morgan Sweeney		1
Alexander M'Ghee	1	Christopher Patterson		1
James M'Grath	1	Hugh Gavaghan		1
James M'Swine	1	Owen Gavaghan		1
John Knox	1	James Black		1
William Cannon	1	Catherine Osburn		1
Robert Montgomery	1	James Graham		1
William M'Loughlin	1	Bartholomew Graham		1
James M'Laughlin	1	William Doolan		1
Matthew Askin	1	Catherine M'Intire		1
William Langin	1	Widow Sweeny		1
John Watson	1	Robert Virtue		1
James Watson	1	William M'Cordack		1
		George Thompson		1
		Daniel Lungan		1

Prsh. of KILLCAR.

	Wheels.			
		William Morrow		1
		William Humphries		1
		Manus M'Corkil		1
Thomas Carscaddin	1	Owen Doolan		1
Daniel M'Breartey	1	Widow Tunney		1
Charles M'Brearty	1	James Tunney		1
John Cochran	1	Andrew Sweeney		1
Andrew Gartlay	1	Petrick Bannagan		1
John Carscaddin	1	Daniel Ash		1
Thomas Lenaghan	1	William Kerrigan		1
Denis Cannon	1	Francis Moore		1
Patrick M'Brearty	1	Edward Kelly		1
Charles M'Fadden	1	John Kelly		1
James Cannon	1	Daniel Dougherty		1
Connell M'Intire	1	James Gallaugher		1
		John Hills		1
		Owen Hills		1

Prsh. of KILBARRON.

	Wheels.			
		John Patten		1
		John Patten		1
James Clurey	4	William Patten		1
Adam King	4	John Patten		1
John White	4	Francis Kerrigan		1
James Gallaugher	3	Owen Kerrigan		1
Owen Gallaugher	3	Daniel Cusack		1
John M'Que	3	James Green		1
John Miles	2	William Green		1
Thomas M'Cawley	2	Widow Connolly		1
Michael Lungan	2	James Monaghan		1
Terence M'Cormack	2	Thomas Monaghan		1
Francis Tunney	2	William Lipsitt		1
Owen Tunney	2	Thomas Lipsitt		1
Thomas Tunney	2	Michael Lipsitt		1

Abstract from 'Spinning Wheel Premium Entitlement Lists'
(1796) see p. 40.

1740: Protestant Householders:

Parishes of Clonmany, Culdaff, Desertegney, Donagh, Fawne (Fahan), Moville, Templemore (Mintiaghs or Barr of Inch). Christian and surnames in respective townlands. GO 539

1760-1769: Freeholders Lists:

People who held land for life as distinct from leaseholders and annual rent payers. They were a major group entitled to vote. NLI. m/f P. 975; PRONI. T. 808/14999.

1761-1788: Freeholder Lists:

NLI. ms 787/8

1766: Donaghmore Parish Census:

NAI. M 207/8. Inch, Leck Protestant Census: NAI 1A 41 100 and in 'The Laggan and its Presbyterianism' Leck. 1905.

1770: Freeholders Entitled to Vote:

NLI. ms 987-88.

1782: Inhabitants of Culdaff Parish:

In 'Three Hundred Years in Inishowen', A. Young 1929.

1794: Householders in St. Johnston:

Tenants of the Abercorn Estate In 'The Laggan and its Presbyterianism' Leck. 1905.

1796: Spinning Wheel Premium Entitlement Lists:

In order to encourage the linen industry the Irish Linen Board awarded free spinning wheels to people growing certain acreages of flax. The names of people receiving spinning wheels in their respective parishes are listed. NAI. m/fiche, NLI Ir63341117. (see p. 39)

1799: Templecrone Protestant Householders:

In 'Irish Ancestor' 16(2) 1984. 78-79.

1799: Muster Roll:

PRONI T. 115B

1802-1803: Culdaff Parish; Protestant Census:

In 'Three Hundred Years of Inishowen' A. Young. 1929

1820-1830's: Tithe Applotment Books:

Tax levied by the Church of Ireland on all occupiers of land from 1823. The 'Books' recorded those people liable to pay, the amount and the acreage of land. Tithepayers are listed in their parish and townland. NLI. m/f; NAI. m/f; Gilbert Library, Dublin (m/f).

1831– National Schools: Pupil Registers (See p. 69)

1857: Primary Valuation of Tenements or Griffith's Valuations (See p. 55)

1901: Government Census:

These are the original returns in bound volume form of a comprehensive census of all households in the country. They list all persons living at a specific address at the time of the Census. Personal details for each person in the household include name, surname, age, relationship (e.g. Wife, son) married or single, religion, occupation, place born (county or town), ability to read, write and speak English and Irish. NAI; Co. DON. LIB. (m/film). An index to the Census Records for Co, Donegal is planned by Largy Books, P.O. Box 6023, Fort McMurray, Alberta T9H 4W1, Canada.

1911: Government Census:

These are the original returns which are in unbound form in boxes. They include the same details as the 1901 Census and also note how many years a couple were married, plus how many children were born to them and how many survived. There are also details on the residence and the 'offices' (i.e. outhouses) attached to the main house (e.g. barn, shed, stable etc.) NAI; CO. DON. LIB. (m/film).

1936: Electoral Registers:

In bound volume form. These are the earliest and most complete available. They include everyone 21 years and over in their respective townlands or street addresses. NLI Ref: Ir324 R2

Poor Law Unions (and Superintendent Registrar's Districts, see p. 44) of
Donegal

Chapter 7   Civil Registration of Birth, Death and Marriage

Civil registration of births, marriages and deaths of all denominations in Ireland started in 1864. However, Church of Ireland marriages had been registered from 1845. Prior to this time there are no records of these events other than in church records.

In the system for Civil Registration, Registrars were appointed in districts based on the Poor Law Unions (see p. 18). Each District compiled its own records, which were sent to a General Register Office (GRO) in Dublin in which all records were stored. An index to all of the records in each year is available in the GRO, and an index to the records in each district is also available at the District offices.

Although a system for registration was established in 1864, there was no penalty for non-registration until 1874. Births in particular may not have been registered. For Catholics, baptism was a sacrament and considered more important than registration of a birth. Thus baptismal records are probably more comprehensive.

Birth Certificate: A full certificate states date, place of birth and when registered; name/surname of child; name/surname of father, his address and occupation; name/surname/maiden name of mother; name/surname and address of informant.

Marriage Certificate: The certificate states date and place of marriage (including church); name, surname and ages of bride and groom ; condition (e.g. bachelor, widow etc); occupations; addresses; names/surnames and occupations of fathers of each; witnesses names/surnames; name of officiating minister.

Death Certificate: The certificate states date and place of death and when registered; name/surname of deceased; condition (e.g.. married, widow etc) ; age; occupation; cause of death; name/surname and address of informant.

The official lay-out of certificates may suggest that the content is definitive. However, it is wise to remember that the information is only as accurate as the informant caused it to be.

All certificates state the county, the Registration District and the Superintendent Registrar's District. The Registration District corresponds to the Dispensary District of the Poor Law Union and the Superintendent Registrar's District corresponds to the Poor Law Union area. When consulting the GRO indexes for a birth etc it is important to know the area covered by the Superintendent Registrar's District. It is also useful to note that these often cross both parish and county borders.

The "Index to the Townlands and Towns" (see p. 18) gives the PLU location and therefore the Superintendent Registrar's District location of each townland in Donegal.

The Superintendent Registrar sent certified copies of the registers to the GRO in Dublin. However, the Superintendent Registrar indexed each register within his jurisdiction while the GRO compiled birth, marriage and death indexes for all of Ireland. In the GRO only indexes can be searched whereas at the county registry offices the original register books can be searched by the public.

From 1922 the new Northern Irish state kept separate registers from the Free State. Both the GRO (Dublin) and the GRO (Belfast) charge for consulting indexes and obtaining certificates.

The LDS have extensive microfilms both of indexes and certificates from the GRO. They can be searched at their Family History Centres in Dublin, Belfast and elsewhere in the world.

The Mormon Church headquarters are at Salt Lake City, Utah in the USA. They have been collecting genealogical material since 1894. Their interest in tracing ancestors is to posthumously baptize them into the Mormon Church. Whatever their motives the continuing result of their work is a vast collection of genealogical records. Millions of ancestors names are contained on microfilm, microfiche and computer data-bases.

From 1948 the Mormon Church began microfilming Irish genealogical material including baptisms and marriage registers of all denominations. However, not all registers or parishes were covered as they were restricted in their filming by the churches involved.

The Mormon Church produced the International Genealogical Index (IGI) for countries world-wide including Ireland. Its accessible form is on microfiche which is indexed by county and surname. It is useful when tracing uncommon surnames or as a surname index when neither the county or parish are known. Once a family is identified it is possible to construct a family tree from the data. The IGI also include GRO birth and marriage entries.

One of the aims of the Mormon Church is to have Family History Centres attached to all their churches worldwide. At present in Ireland these are in Dublin and Belfast. Access is free as is the viewing of the material.

The LDS collection of GRO microfilms (Jan 1995) is as follows.

LDS Family History Centre - GRO Microfilms - Irish Republic

Births:	Indexes	1864-1958
	Certificates	1864-1881; 1880-1910; 1930-1955
Marriages:	Indexes	1845-1958
	Certificates	1845-1870
Deaths:	Indexes	1864-1958
	Certificates	1864-1870

Northern Ireland (6 Counties)*

Births:	Indexes	1864-1959
	Certificates:	1864-1881; 1900-1910; 1922-1959
Marriages:	Indexes	1845-1959
	Certificates	1845-1870; 1922-1959
Deaths:	Indexes	1864-1959
	Certificates	1864-1870; 1922-1959

* NB. From 1922 the new Northern Irish State began to
keep separate registers from the Irish Republic.

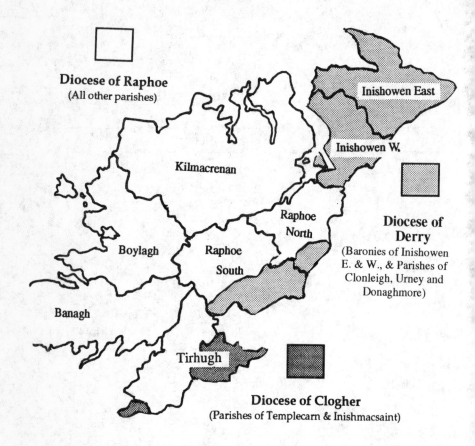

Diocese of Raphoe
(All other parishes)

Inishowen East

Inishowen W.

Kilmacrenan

Raphoe
North

Diocese of
Derry
(Baronies of Inishowen
E. & W., & Parishes of
Clonleigh, Urney and
Donaghmore)

Boylagh

Raphoe
South

Banagh

Tirhugh

Diocese of Clogher
(Parishes of Templecarn & Inishmacsaint)

Donegal Baronies and Church of Ireland Dioceses

Chapter 8   Wills & Administrations

A will is a legal expression of a person's wishes in regard to distribution of their property after their death. By making a will a person can ensure that property and money are left to persons of their choice. Because wills often mention many people in a family, and also properties associated with the family, they can be very useful sources of family history.

The process of legalising a will is known as Probate. The instructions contained within the will cannot legally be acted upon until the will is proved.The Probate Court will usually appoint an executor to implement the instructions in the will, and generally the person appointed will be the person nominated by the deceased in the will itself.

Where a person dies intestate (ie without making a will), or where the will cannot be executed as requested (eg if the specified executor has also died), the Probate court must itself ensure a proper distribution of the person's estate. An Administration is the court's decision as to distribution of the property of a person who dies intestate. Although less useful than wills, these are also useful documents for determining immediate family connections.

Before 1858 the Church of Ireland was responsible for Probate. In each Church of Ireland diocese there was a Consistorial court which proved the will of the residents within the diocese. If the resident had estate valued over £5 in a second diocese, the will needed to be proved at the Prerogative Court of the Archbishop of Armagh. One common circumstance of this was where their land crossed the border of the diocese. Wills proved in this court tended to be made by the wealthier strata of Irish society.

The 1857 Probate Act transferred Probate jurisdiction from the Church of Ireland to a new court of Probate. A Principal Registry was established in Dublin which also functioned as the new Prerogative Court. Eleven District Registries functioning as Consistorial Courts were located in the rest of the country. County Donegal was covered by the Londonderry District Registry.

The history of Irish wills, like some other genealogical sources, has been unfortunate as much of the original will material was stored in the PRO when the building was destroyed in the 1922 Civil War. The bulk of the Prerogative wills, Consistorial Wills, & Administration Bonds and Will Books were destroyed, although all the indexes were saved.

The National Archives has made extensive efforts since 1922 to locate wills and copies of wills. Extant wills or copies are listed in the Card Index of the Search Room and this index is continually being supplemented.

Terms

Abstract: The main details of an original will or administration are executor's name and names of beneficiaries.

Administration: When the deceased had not made a will either the Prerogative or Consistorial court decided on the allocation of the estate and appointed an administrator to execute their decision.

Administrator: Person appointed by the court to distribute the deceased person's estate when no will had been made. Normally a relative did this.

Estate: The property of a deceased person.

Executor: Person appointed by the court to implement the instructions in the will, normally a family member.

Grant Books: The administrator entered a bond for a sum of money to ensure he carried out wishes of the court. No bonds survive but an index for them is contained in the Grant Books.

Index: These give deceased Christian, Surname, Address and year of will/ administration.

Intestate: When a person died without making a will.

Probate: Process by which a court declares the will to be legally binding.

Testator: The person who makes the will.

Material	Period	Location	Comments
Prerogative Wills	1536-1800	NAI-(note books) PRONI + GO (sketch pedigrees)	Wm Betham abstracts
Prerogative Administrations	1536-1800	NAI-(note books) PRONI + GO (sketch pedigrees)	

186   *Raphoe Wills, 1684-1858.*

				Date of Probate.
Mountgomery, David, Manfad	..	..	..	*1707
,, John, Monfàd	..	..	..	*1725
Mountgumry, Robert, Brenter	..	..	..	*1711
Mungomrie, Alexr., Ray	..	..	..	*1715
,, *See also* Montgomery *and* Montgomry.				
Mulcartagh, John, Glasboley	..	..	..	1801
Mulchartaugh, Michael	..	..	..	1790
Muldoon, John, Duballah ..	..	..	..	1815
Mulharin, Philip, Rossnawlaugh	..	..	..	1842
Mulkeran, Denis, Glasboly..	..	..	..	1812
Mulloy, John, Rathriagh	..	..	..	1763
Mulreany, James, Drumlaughtafin ..	..	..	*1810
Munro, Wm. (Rev.), Curate of Raymochy	..	..	*1715
Munteeth, Robert	..	..	..	1728
Murphy, Darby, Mannor Cunningham	..	..	*1796
Murray, Catherine, Drumbarnet	..	..	..	1806
,, John, Gartan	..	..	..	*1718
,, ,, Maghrihober	..	..	..	1739
,, ,, Drumbarnett	..	..	..	1851
,, Richard (surgeon), Ballyshannon (*entry in Will book only*)	..	..	..	1833
Murrey, Hugh, Creven	..	..	..	*1739
Murry, Denis, p. Conwall ..	..	..	..	1803

————

NESBITT, John, p. Killybegs	..	..	..	1731
,, ,, Liskerren	..	..	..	1800
,, Mary, Lough Hill (*copy*)	..	..	..	1836
,, Robert, Ramelton	..	..	..	1794
,, *See also* Nisbitt.				
Nicholl, William, Little Veagh	..	..	..	1804
Nimo, *als.* Bates, Alison *or* Eleanor. *See* Bates.				
Nisbitt, Alexander, Tillydonnell	..	..	..	*1717
,, Charles (Rev.), Greenhills ..	..	..	1835
,, Elizabeth, Tillydonnell	..	..	..	*1758
,, Mary ..	..	..	..	1835
,, *See also* Nesbitt.				
Noble, Alexander..	..	..	..	1727
,, Thomas, Broadpath	..	..	..	1787

**Index to Consistorial Wills in Raphoe Diocese,
Gertrude Thrift.** (See p. 50)

Material	Period	Location	Comments
Prerogative Wills Books	1664-1684 1706-1708 (A-W) 1726-1729 (A-W) 1777(A-L) 1813(K-Z) 1834(A-E)	NAI	Also noted in "A Guide to Copies & Abstracts of Irish Wills"
Prerogative Administration Grants Day Books	1684-1688 1748-1751 1839 1784-1788	NAI NAI	
Consistorial Wills (Vol 5)	Derry Diocese 1612-1858 Raphoe Diocese 1684-1858	NAI NAI	Gertrude Thrift Vol 5. Pub by Phillimore 1920
Consistorial Administration Bonds-Indexes	Derry Diocese 1698-1857 Raphoe Diocese 1684-1858	NAI NAI	
Consistorial Grant Books	1812-1851 Derry & Raphoe Diocese	NAI	Damaged - not for public viewing
Wills Index District Registry of Londonderry	1858-1899	NAI PRONI (m/f 15c)	Any extant wills or copies in NAI or PRONI. NB. Index 1858-1877 in one volume
Original Donegal Wills	1900-1921		PRONI
Testamentary Card Index		NAI	If a will or copy exists it should be noted on a card.

Additional Sources

Index to Prerogative Wills of Ireland; 1536-1810; Arthur Vicars 1897

Index to Will Abstracts at GO in 'Analecta Hibernica 17'; 1949; Article by P. Beryl Eustace.

Abstracts of Wills at Registry of Deeds; 1708-1745 (vol 1); P. Beryl Eustace
1746-1788 (vol 2)   "
1785-1832 (vol 3); P. Beryl Eustace
& Eilis
Ellis. 1984.

Abstracts of Wills of Irish Testators at; NLI Ms. 1397

The Prerogative Court of Canterbury; 1639-1698

Raphoe/Derry Diocese Wills in 'Three Hundred Years in Inishowen'; Amy Young
Ref. NLI Ir 9292y1

Abstracts of Wills of Irish Testators at the Prerogative Court of Canterbury; 1639-1698.
Ref: NLI Ms. 1397

Abstracts made by Protestant Clergy & their Families (18th century); RCBL

Indexes to Irish Will Registers; Inland Revenue 1828-1879; NAI
Irish Will Registers; 1828-1839
Indexes to Irish Administration Registers; 1828-1879; NAI
Irish Administration Registers; 1829-1839; NB. Made by people with property in Ireland & England.

Indexes to Wills in Land Commission (mainly late 19th century); NLI
This material is held by the Land Commission which is based in same building as NAI.

Leslie Collection; NLI - ref. m/f P.799
Ainsley Will Abstracts; GO ref 535 & 631
Wilson Collection; NLI. ref m/f P.1990
Welply Collection; in RCBL and indexed in 'Irish Genealogist' 1985/86

110 LANE, PATRICK, Castlefin, parish of Donaghmore, Co. Donegal, innholder. 29 Feb. 1792. Precis ¾ p. 28 April 1792.

To his beloved wife Jane Lane his freehold tenement lands in Knockramer [? Co. Donegal] and all his furniture; five shillings and five pence to all his daughters Elizth. McGlaghlin, Margt. Wallace and Jane Coyle in full of what they might demand as being his children.

Witnesses: Jas. Simms, innkeeper, Joseph Mahon, weaver, both of Castlefinn, and John Sime, Tamnacrum, gent., in said Co. Donegal.

Memorial witnessed by: said John Sime and Peter McDonagh, city of Londonderry, notary public.

447, 171, 289658   Jane Coyle (seal)
                                    daughter, her mark.
                          Jane Lane also being deceased.
                    Sworn at Londonderry 16 April 1792.

Chapter 9   Land Records

The major sources relating to land ownership and tenure in Ireland can be found in the records of the Registry of Deeds, Land Commission, NAI, NLI and in private collections.

Establishing the landowner's name or title is essential in order to discover the location of the property and what records pertain to it. The Marquis of Donegal had the surname Chichester and when the male line died out the estates passed by marriage to the Earl of Shaftesbury. The documents relating to the estates therefore could be located under the name Marquis of Donegal, Chichester or the Earl of Shaftesbury. The Primary Valuation can be used to find the names of landlords, middlemen and tenants in the mid 19th century (see p. 55). Other useful reference sources are:-

Lewis's Topographical Dictionary of Ireland.
> S.Lewis. London 1837
> - Lists the principal landlords and residents in each Irish civil parish and town

Landowners of Ireland. 1876
> - Lists major landowners

The Landlords of Ireland.
> O.H.Hussey de Burgh, 1878
> - Lists landlords owning 500 acres or more.

Analecta Hibernica.
> Numbers 15 (1944); 20(1958); 23(1966); 25(1967); 32(1985).
> - Lists estate records already indexed.

General Alphabetical Index to the Townlands and Towns, Parishes and Baronies of Ireland.
> Thom's. Dublin. 1861.

RAMELTON, a market and post-town, in the parish of AUGHNISH, barony of KILMACRENAN, county of DONEGAL, and province of ULSTER, 19 miles (N. N. W.) from Lifford, and 123½ (N. W. by N.) from Dublin; containing 1783 inhabitants. Sir Wm. Stewart, Knt., who was much in favour with Jas. I., became an undertaker for the plantation of escheated lands, of which he obtained a grant or patent of 1000 acres in this vicinity, and was created a baronet of Ireland in 1623. At the time of Pynnar's Survey he had built a strong bawn here, 80 feet square and 16 feet high, with four flankers and a strong and handsome castle ; and contiguous to these he had built the town, then containing 45 houses, inhabited by 57 British families ; he had also nearly completed the erection of a church : the place was then considered well situated for military defence. The town stands on the river Lenon, which here empties itself into Lough Swilly, and is navigable for small vessels : it consists of three streets, containing 341 houses, and is admirably adapted for manufactures of every description. Here are extensive corn-mills, a brewery, bleach-green, and linen manufactory, and a considerable quantity of linen is made by hand in the vicinity. A market for provisions is held on Tuesday, and on Thursday and Saturday for corn ; and fairs are held on the Tuesday next after May 20th, Nov. 15th, and on the Tuesday after Dec. 11th. A chief constabulary police force is stationed in the town, and petty sessions are held on alternate Thursdays. There is a small salmon fishery, producing about £500 annually ; the fish are considered to be in season throughout the year, and are mostly exported to England. In the town are the parochial church, meeting-houses for Presbyterians in connection with the Synod of Ulster (of the first class) and for Methodists, a small fever hospital, and a dispensary. A loan fund has been established ; also a ladies' society and a shop for the sale of clothes at reduced prices to the poor. The parochial and Presbyterian schools, noticed in the article on Aughnish, are also in the town. On the shore of Lough Swilly is Fort Stewart, the residence of Sir Jas. Stewart, Bart., surrounded by an extensive and well planted demesne ; and at a short distance to the north-east is Fort Stewart Castle, erected by Sir Wm. Stewart, the original patentee of the surrounding lands. Pearls of considerable value are occasionally found in the river Lenon.

The entry for Ramelton in Lewis's Topographical Dictionary of Ireland
Lewis, Samuel, 1839

Griffith's Valuation.

Under the Tenement Act (1842), a national system of land taxation was introduced. This was based on an estimation of the valuation of the land or property of each landholder or householder. To establish the names of the tax-payers, and the valuation of their holdings, a survey of all land-holders was conducted in the 1840's and '50's. This 'Primary Valuation of Tenements' was supervised by Richard Griffith and is usually referred to as 'Griffith's Valuation'. It provides the landholders names and various information on their holdings, within each county, barony, poor law union, civil parish and townland. Details provided include the townland, householder/landholder name, the name of the landlord (Immediate Lessor), acreage, valuation, Ordnance Survey map reference and Valuation Office map reference.

The names of tenants and lessors changed over time and the changes were recorded by the Valuation Office. "Griffith's Valuation' occasionally noted other interesting details such as the fathers of male tenants (as a basis for distinguishing between people of the same name), husbands of female tenants; nicknames and occasionally occupations. Functions of specific buildings, e.g. churches, schools, graveyards, barracks, RIC stations, cornmills, forges, inns and shops were also noted. Tenure, House and Field Books were also compiled as part of the original Valuation. Of these the Tenure Books are the most useful as they note the tenant's annual rent and lease duration.

An index to the Griffith Valuation was compiled in the 1960's by the National Library. The 'Index of Surnames' lists all the surnames found in the Valuation and the Tithe Books. The index can be useful in determining where in a county persons of a particular surname lived. 'The Index of Surnames is available in book form in the NLI, National Archives and on microfiche in county libraries and other repositories.

Registry of Deeds

The Registry of Deeds was established in 1708 for the registering of all land transactions e.g. conveyance, mortgages and leases. Marriage settlements and wills were also registered as if they were deeds. The deeds were transcribed or abstracts were made from them and written up into large volumes (the original deeds are stored in vaults). The volumes can be accessed using a 'Names Index' (grantors) and a 'Land Index' (county, barony and townland). The reference numbers in the indexes can be used to locate the relevant volume and thus a transcript of the abstract.

The ethos behind the establishment of the Registry of Deeds was to prevent land passing into Catholic ownership and Catholics are not usually found in the volumes until the Penal Laws were relaxed in 1778. After this date more

Catholic landholders registered their deeds. In general registered deeds were made between people of equal economic standing and it is unlikely that the mass of small tenant farmers would have registered deeds.

Estate Records

Estate record material may amount to thousands of documents with the majority relating to the estate owners. However some documents such as rent ledgers contain lists of tenants on the estate from a period of many years.

By the close of the 18th century, estate records had generated a miscellany of documents including maps, tenant lists, rentals, letters, lease books, employment records on workers and account books. More tenants in general were being mentioned by the start of the 19th century. Tenant rental lists and leases can be used to link ancestors who lived at the close of the 18th century and the start of the 19th century.

168

VALUATION OF TENEMENTS.

PARISH OF FAHAN, LOWER.

No. and Letters of Reference to Map.	Townlands and Occupiers. Names.	Immediate Lessors.	Description of Tenement.	Area. A. R. P.	Rateable Annual Valuation. Land. £ s. d.	Buildings. £ s. d.	Total Annual Valuation of Rateable Property. £ s. d.
	STRANCLEA — *continued.*						
3	Henry M'Loughlin, sen.	George Harvey	House, office, and land	70 1 19	3 0 0	0 10 0	2 10 0
4	Anthony Donaghy	Same	House, offices, and land	152 1 30	6 15 0	0 10 0	7 5 0
5	John Donaghy	Same	House, offices, and land	47 2 30	3 0 0	0 10 0	3 10 0
			Total	380 0 29	21 1 0	2 9 0	23 10 0
	FALLASK (*Ord. S. 19.*)						
1	Michael M'Kenny	George Harvey	House, offices, and land	95 1 16	5 8 0	0 12 0	6 0 0
2	Henry M'Kenny	Same	House, offices, and land	453 2 3	13 5 0	0 15 0	14 0 0
3	Michael Crossan	Henry M'Kenny	House and land	4 2 24	1 5 0	0 5 0	1 10 0
4	John M'Devitt	George Harvey	House, office, and land	131 0 24	5 5 0	0 5 0	5 10 0
5	Charles Donaghy	Same	House, offices, and land	78 0 30	3 12 0	0 3 0	3 15 0
6	John M'Loughlin	Same	House, offices, and land	112 3 20	5 5 0	0 10 0	5 15 0
7	Michael M'Loughlin	Same	House, office, and land	114 0 16	4 13 0	0 7 0	5 0 0
			Total	1609 3 13	38 18 0	2 12 0	41 10 0
	OWENBOY (*Ord. S. 19 & 20*)						
1	Edward Carey	George Harvey	House, offices, and land	103 0 10	8 18 0	0 12 0	9 10 0
2	Thomas Carey	Same	House, offices, and land	361 2 11	10 5 0	0 10 0	10 15 0
3	Henry Carey	Same	Land	317 3 11	7 15 0	—	7 15 0
4	William M'Loughlin	Same	House, offices, and land	563 1 0	15 5 0	0 15 0	16 0 0
5	Michael M'Kenny	Same	Land	375 1 1	9 10 0	—	9 10 0
			Total	2023 3 33	51 13 0	1 17 0	53 10 0
	CONNAGHIN.						

Return from the Parish of Fahan from Griffith's Valuation

Co. Donegal Estate Papers

Estate	Place	Record	Source
William Connolly	Ballyshannon Estate	Tenants names/ holdings 1718,1726	Don. Ann. 1981
Earl of Leitrim	Kilmacrenan	Rentals 1858- 1869	NLI Ms 5175- 5178
Thomas Connolly	Drumholm, Donegal	Sale/rentals	NLI 347/15
Henry Bruen, HG Cooper, See Connolly	Ballyshannon		
A. Murray-Stewart	Killymard, Killybegs Killaughtee, Kilcar Inishkeel, Tullyaughnish	Rentals 1842,1845	NLI Ms 5465-66
H.G. Murray– Stewart	Killymard, Killybegs Killaughtee, Kilcar Inishgale	Rentals 1847- 1859	NLI Ms 5467- 5476
H.G. Murray– Stewart	"	Rentals 1852, '65, '76, '80, '85-'6, 1890-91, 1869-70	Donegal County Archive (see p. 84/86)
Hart Family	Kilderry	Rental/cash account 1757-1767, 1796-1803	NLI Ms 7885
Mary Broughton	Estate	Tenant List 1730	Don. Ann. 1977
Leslie Estate	Pettigo	Rentals 1777- 1800, 1820- 1823,	NLI Ms 55810-12
Lecky Estate	Ballinacor	Rentals 1846-1900	PRONI

Musgrave Estate	Banagh Barony	Map/tenant list 1856-1866	NLI Ms
Castle Grove Estate		Rentals 1840-1844	NLI m/f P.975
Harvey Estate	Gortfad	Rentals 1820-1920	
Irwin Estate	Mucketty, Letter, Kilmacrenan	Maps/rentals 19th century	NAI
Irish & Scotch Estates		Account Books 1859-61; Receivers Rental 1852 with 1,614 names	Donegal County Archive (see p. 84/86)
Clements, Robert		Maps of Estate (1779) with names of Lessees	Donegal County Archive (see p. 84/86)
Burton, Irwin		Valuation of Estate (1882 -3) with names of tenants	Donegal County Archive (see p. 84/86)
Conyngham Estate	Stranorlar	Rentals 1700-1920	NLI
Marquis of Donegal {Shaftsbury Papers}	Inishowen Barony	Maps/rentals 19th century	PRONI

Encumbered Estate Records

Many estates in the 19th century were bankrupt and sold by auction to pay debts. Owners of large estates were only too pleased to sell off parts or all of their estate but this process could take time. The Encumbered Estates Act of 1849 eased this process by the establishment of the Encumbered Estates Court. In the 1849-1857 period about 3,000 estates were sold. Surviving records include publicity bills which included details of the estates often with the principal tenants names and the basis of their lease.

Land Commission

The Land Commission was established in 1881 and its main purpose was to fix fair rents when disputes existed between landlords and tenants. The ILC also made loans to tenants who wanted to improve or purchase their land. The ILC needed to be satisfied that a tenant's land could be improved and that a tenant was financially able to repay a loan. To this end inspectors were appointed to visit properties to ascertain these matters. This information is contained with the 'Inspector's Records'.

Edward Keane of the NLI researched material for 9343 estates and compiled a card index (available on open access at the NLI). It comprises of 1) 'Topographical Index' by county, barony and vendor's name. 2) 'Name Index' by vendor's name, estate location and estate number. Using the estate number a description of estate documents can be found in bound volumes. The most useful genealogical information are the tenant rental lists.

Land Commission (same building as the National Archives-appointment necessary).

Below is an example of a Land Commission record in the National Library

Index	Card Ref	Landlord/Estate	Guide to Material in Box
Vol LC 474/	Box 560	George Miller Harvey Inishowen West & East	Deed Sir Arthur Chichester to Richard O'Dougherty 1610 Rory O'Doughertie to John Harvey 1696. Deeds1769-1890 Rentals 1872 & 1889.

Congested Districts Board

The Land Act (1891) established the CDB in a number of counties including County Donegal. The CDB was responsible for the redistribution of land and the relocation of tenants. It also developed local industries, agriculture and fisheries.

Edward Keane of the National Library prepared a volume on the estates within the CDB areas entitled the (annual) Reports of the Congested Districts Board. The reports contain accounts of the work of the CDB in detail.

Chapter 10　Newspapers

The first newspaper established in County Donegal was the Ballyshannon Herald in 1831 which was both conservative and unionist in outlook. As a counterblast the Liberator was launched also in Ballyshannon in 1839 but it lasted only a short time. No further newspapers were published within Co. Donegal until 1885 when the Donegal Independent was first issued. However, the newspapers published in the adjoining county of Derry also covered events in Co. Donegal and are an additional source of local history.

Newspapers are a source of many different types of information. Apart from notices of birth, marriage and death, they also named individuals involved in political upheavals, accidents and other newsworthy events. They also published names and addresses of people convicted of crimes, the type of offence and the sentence. They also occasionally published names and addresses of people for various civil or legal purposes eg those intending to register freeholds to the Quarter Sessions in order to be able to vote.

For East Donegal people, Derry was a major port of embarkation, commercial centre and marketing outlet. Advertisments for shops, trades and hotels begin to appear in the latter half of the 19th century and these can help to locate and identify individuals involved in various trades and commercial activities.

Births, marriages and deaths were virtually always listed, but they tended to be placed by the wealthier section of society.

Copies of Donegal newspapers are available in Donegal County Library, the National Library (NLI), the British Library (BL) and in some other archives.

Donegal and Derry Newspapers

Title	Published	Founded	Location
Ballyshannon Herald	Ballyshannon	1831	NLI, BL
The Liberator	Ballyshannon	1839	NLI, BL
Donegal Independent	Ballyshannon	1885	NLI, BL
Donegal Vindicator	Ballyshannon	1906	NLI, BL
Donegal Democrat	Ballyshannon	1919	NLI, BL
Londonderry Journal	Derry	1772-1866	NLI
continued as *Derry Journal*		1866	NLI, BL
Londonderry Chronicle	Derry	1829	NLI, BL
Londonderry Standard	Derry	1853-1880	NLI, BL
continued as *Derry Standard*			
Londonderry Sentinel	Derry	1885-1974	NLI, BL
continued as *Derry Sentinel*		1974	NLI
Derry People	Derry	1902	NLI, BL

NB:- Other counties bordering Co. Donegal also have newpapers that start in the late 19th century.

No Armes
_____

[f182ᵛ] Barony de Rapho
The Lady Conningham Widdow of Sir James Conningham,
undertaker of 2,000 acres, her men and armes.

William Conningham
James Calquahan
Andrew mcCorkill
John mcCorkill
Tobias Hood
James Davye
Peter Starret
John mcquchowne
James Knox
Adam Garvance

Swords and Pikes
_____

James mcAdowe
ffyndlay Ewing
Dunkan mcffarlan
Ninian ffoulton
James Scot
William Rankin
Daniell Ramsay
Martin Galbreath
Patrick Porter

Swords and Snaphances
_____

William mcIltherne
David Walker
John Barbor

Swords and Calleuers
_____

James Makee

Sword and halbert
_____

f183   Andrew George
James mcIlman
Michaell Rot(h?)es
Patrick Miller
Robert Muntgomery
Alexander Conningham

Richard Leaky
Robert Staret
John mcIihome
Sallomon Giffin
David Reed
Donnell mcDonnell
Alexander Carlell
William Gafeth

Swords onely
_____

Gilbert Highgate
Patrick Porter
Robert Hasta
William Gambell
John Hunter
John Crawfford
Robert Johnston
Henry Smyth
William Boyes
David Ramsay
William Steward
Robert Crafford
[f183ᵛ] James Conningham
Andrew Conningham
John Crafford
John Hunter
John Wilson
James Bredyne
Mungo Davy
William Richey
John mcIlhome
Henry Hunter
John mcHutchon
James Rankin
William Killy
Robert Pots
William Gambell
John Lyone
James Knox   66

Extract from a County Donegal Muster Roll of 1630 showing the fighting men
available to Lady Conningham, an undertaker in the Barony of Raphoe, and
their arms. From Donegal Annual 10(2) (1972). (See p. 38)

Chapter 11   Commercial Directories

Commercial Directories were produced by private publishers as listings of tradesmen, professionals and gentry in different areas. Many of them also contained other useful local information (e.g. police, militia, court sessions, mail-coaches timetables etc).

These directories provide information useful both to the local historian and genealogist.

The first directories of the 18th century tended to cover only Dublin and its environs but by the 19th century the directories had begun to cover all of Ireland.

Pigot & Co's directories published from 1824 cover many Irish towns and are augmented both in places and people, by Slater's directories and by Thom's Directory from 1845.

Many towns and villages of County Donegal are described in detail in both Pigots and Slater's Directories. They contained such information as parish, railway stations, churches, constabulary, courts, dispensaries and forts. As well as gentry and clergy, many tradesmen are noted under various headings.

To take 'Slater's 1870 Directory of Ireland' entry for Buncrana and Clonmany as an example, the range of traders listed include Bakers, Blacksmiths, Boot & Shoe Makers, Butchers, Butter & Egg Merchants, Carpenters & Cart makers, China Glass & Earthenware Dealers, Emigration Agents, Flax & Tow Spinners, Grocers, Hardware-men, Leather Sellers, Linen & Woollen Drapers & Haberdashers, Milliners & Dressmakers, Painters & Glaziers, Physicians & Surgeons, Saddlers & Harness Makers, Seed & Guano Merchants, Shirt Agents, Spirit & Porter Dealers, Tailors, Timber, Coal, Iron & Slate Merchants.

Under 'miscellaneous' is found Cornmiller, Whitesmith, Coroner, Straw Bonnet Maker and Dyer & Cleaner.

These Directories are available in many libraries. The original directories can be examined in the National Library of Ireland, and in some other archives. Pigot's Directory (1824) and Slater's Directories for 1846, 1856, 1870, 1881 & 1894 are also on microfiche at the National Library and county libraries.

LETTERKENNY

Is a considerable market and post town in the county of Donegal, on the banks of the Swilly, one hundred and thirteen miles north-north-west of Dublin, thirty-four north by east of Ballyshannon, twenty-one and a half north by east of Donegal, and six north-west of Raphoe. Within half a mile is Port Balliraine, whither vessels of one hundred tons bring iron, salt, colonial produce, &c., and whence they export hides, butter, &c. This is the market for a very considerable tract of country; the principal commodities sold here are linen, yarn, cattle, and provisions. The town consists of one tolerably well built street, and commands a view of the country around for a considerable distance. Letterkenny possesses a parish church, a Catholic chapel, no less than three dissenting meeting houses, a dispensary, and a good market house, over which the general quarter sessions are held twice in the year. The market day is Friday, and fairs are held on the Friday before Candlemas day, the Friday before St. Patrick's day, Good Friday, the 12th of May, Friday before the 12th of August, the 8th of November, and the Friday before Christmas. The Population is near 2,000.

POST OFFICE.—*Post Master*, Mr. James Foy. The Dublin mail is despatched at eleven at night to Raphoe, and arrives at thirteen minutes past seven in the evening. The Dunfanaughy mail leaves this office at a quarter past seven on Sundays, Wednesdays and Fridays, and returns on Sundays, Tuesdays and Thursdays. Office hours from seven in the morning till eleven at night

GENTRY AND CLERGY.

Boyd Alex. esq, Gortlee
Boyd John, esq, Ballymacool
Boyd Rer. Wm. Kiltoey
Brooke Thos. esq, Castle-grove
Chambers Dan. esq, Rock-hill
Chambers Rev. John, Woodville
Gamble Rev. —
Homan Rev. Geo. Barn-hill
Leyttle Rev. Joseph
Lighton W. H. M. esq, Drum-lodge
Mansfield Francis, esq, Castle-wray
Mc Gettigan Rev. Patrick
Spratt Rev. Andrew
Stofford Rev. Dr. Joseph, rector, Glendoon
Wray Wm. esq, Oak Park
Young Ralph, esq, Oatlands

MERCHANTS, TRADESMEN, &c.

ATTORNEYS.

Crawford Charles
Murray Edward

SURGEONS.

Hunter John, (& apothecary)
Patterson John
Reid Thos. (to the dispensary)

MERCHANTS.

Allen Geo. (general)
Gallaghar Jas. (cloth)
King David, (cloth)
Leech Geo. (general)
Moffit Robt. (general)
Peoples Jas. (cloth)
Willson Wm. (general)

SHOPKEEPERS, TRADERS, &c.

Allen Geo. chandler
Blackwood Wm. grocer & chandler
Buckanan Alex. tailor
Caffrey Hugh, publican
Carson John, parish clerk
Clarke Saml. publican
Colonhan Wm. publican
Coran Cornelius, publican
Coyle Henry, publican
Cunningham Saml. saddler
Delap Wm. salt manufacturer
Dobson John, grocer
Elliott John, baker
Ferguson David, druggist
Fisher Wm. grocer, & agent to the Dublin tea company

Foy Jas. ironmonger
Gaily Chas. grocer
Gaily Robt. grocer
Greer Geo. grocer
Hall Saml. painter & glazier
Henderson Gustavus, publican
Hood Henry, grocer
Hunter John & Co, wholesale and retail grocers
Laird Jane, innkeeper
Lynch Hugh, publican
Mc Auley John, painter & glazier
Mc Carran Timothy, woollen draper
Mc Clintock —, publican
Mc Conney Thos. publican
Mc Crea Robt. saddler
Mc Cullum Alex. publican

392

A description of Letterkenny from Pigot's Directory 1824

Commercial Directories of Relevance to Donegal

Pigot's City of Dublin & Hibernian Provincial Directory -1824:

Includes Ballybofey, Ballyshannon, Donegal, Letterkenny, Lifford, Pettigo, Raphoe, Stranorlar.

Pigot's City of Dublin & Hibernian Provincial Directory - 1839

Includes the towns of Ballyshannon, Donegal, Stranorlar, Ballybofey.

Slater's National Commercial Directory of Ireland - 1846:

Includes Ballyshannon, Bundoran, Buncrana, Donegal, Killybegs and Dunkineely, Letterkenny, Lifford and Castlefin, Moville, Raphoe, Ramelton, Stranorlar and Ballybofey.

Henderson's Belfast & Province of Ulster Directory - 1854:

Includes Ballyshannon and Lifford. Further editions in 1856, 1858, 1861, 1863, 1865, 1868, 1870, 1877, 1880, 1884, 1890, 1894, 1900.

Slater's Royal National Commercial Directory of Ireland - 1856

Includes Ballyshannon, Bundoran, Buncrana, Donegal, Killybegs and Dunkineely, Letterkenny, Lifford and Castlefin, Moville, Raphoe, Ramelton, Stranorlar and Ballybofey.

Slater's Directory of Ireland - 1870:

Includes Ballyshannon, Buncrana and Clonmany, Donegal, Dunfanaghy, Glenties and Ardara, Killybegs, Letterkenny and Manorcunningham, Lifford, Moville, Pettigo, Raphoe and Convoy, Ramelton, and Stranorlar.

Slater's Royal National Commercial Directory of Ireland - 1881:

Includes Ballyshannon, Buncrana and Clonmany, Donegal, Dunfanaghy, Glenties and Ardara, Killybegs, Letterkenny and Manorcunningham, Lifford, Moville, Pettigo, Raphoe, Ramelton, Stranorlar and Ballybofey.

Derry Almanac & Directory - 1887:

Includes Ardara, Ballintra, Ballybofey, Ballyshannon, Buncrana, Carndonagh, Carrigans, Castlefin, Donegal, Dunfanaghy, Glenties, Killygordon, Letterkenny, Lifford, Manorcunningham, Milford, Mountcharles, Moville, Raphoe, Ramelton, Rathmullan, Stranorlar, and St. Johnston. (Issued annually from 1891).

Slater's Royal National Commercial Directory of Ireland - 1894

COUNTY OFFICERS.

Clerk of the Crown, J. Joyce, esq., Strabane.
Clerk of the Peace, James Cochran, esq., Crohan House, Lifford.
Deputy Clerk of the Peace, Mr. John Walwood, Stranorlar.
Sessional Crown Solicitor, Wm. Barrett, esq. Riverstown, Ardara.
Treasurer, Francis Mansfield, esq., Castleshanahan, Letterkenny.
Secretary to Grand Jury, S. Sproule, esq., Rathmelton.
County Surveyor, John Stedman, esq., Letterkenny.
Sub-Sheriff, Samuel J. Crookshank, esq., Derry.
Returning Officer, Robert Crookshank, esq., 3, Henrietta-street, Dublin.
Coroner,   *   *   *
Inspector of Weights and Measures, J. Harvey Goory.
Agents for Lloyds. Mr. J. M'Gloin, Ballyshannon; Mr. A. Cassidy, Killybegs; and Mr. R. Coane, Dunfanaghy.

STAMP DISTRIBUTERS.

Head Distributer for the county, Ralph Young, esq., Letterkenny.
Ballybofey, Mrs. King.
Ballyshannon, John Scott.
Donegal, James Mulraney.
Fahan, Mrs. M'Clelland.
Moville, Patrick M'Kinney.
Pettigoe, H. Hamilton.
Ramelton, Jane Hunter.
Raphoe, Samuel Kerr.

BARONY CESS COLLECTORS.

Banagh, I. O'Donnell, Summy, Ardara.
Boylagh, I. O'Donnell, Summy, Ardara
Inishowen east, R. Mitchell, Dunross, Moville.
Inishowen west, J. Dysart, Carnamady, Derry.
Kilmacrenan, William Black, Church-hill.
Raphoe, R. Mansfield, Killygordon.
Tyrhugh, J. Hamilton, Rushbrook, Ballintra.

MILITIA STAFF.

Colonel, Right Hon. the Earl of Leitrim.
Lieutenant-Colonel, E. M. Connolly, esq., M.P.
Major, Sir James Stewart, bart., Fort Stewart.
Adjutant, Samuel Searle.
Agents, Cane & Co., Dublin.

CONSTABULARY OFFICERS.

County Inspector, Henry Townsend, Letterkenny.
Paymaster, James Taylor, Londonderry.

Sub-Inspectors' Stations.

Ballyshannon, Charles Hayden.
Buncrana, Thomas Smith.
Carndonagh, J. C. Wickham.

Dunfanaghy, M. N. Wright.
Glenties, John C. Rodden.
Ramelton, W. Meredith.
Raphoe, A. W. Stafford.

COAST GUARD STATIONS.

Buncrana; Crowris; Dowran; Dunnaff Head; Ennisboffin; Glengad; Guidore; Inniscoo; Loughroris; Malinmore; Mulroy; Port Kenigo; Port Redford; Portnoe; Port Roslin; Rathmullen; Rutland; St. John's point; Sheephaven; Slievebane; Teelin East; Trybane.

MANOR COURTS.

Ballyshannon; Buncrana, Elagh, Green-castle, and Malm; Castlefin; Castle Boyle and Portin Island; Donegal; Kilmacrenan; Killybegs; Magavlin and Lismoghry; Mughrymore; Orwell and Burleigh; Rathmullen; Stranorlar; Termonmagrath; Tyrhugh.

PETTY SESSIONS COURTS.

Place where held, Day, and Name of Clerk.

Ardara, second Tuesday every month; E. Brice.
Ballintra, second Tuesday; A. Jennings.
Ballyshannon, second Wednesday; W. Curry.
Buncrana, second Thursday; C. O'Donnell.
Burnfoot, Churchtown, third Friday every month; H. G. Cairns.
Church-hill, second Tuesday; R. Pearson.
Carndonagh, third Wednesday; G. H. Hewston.
Cotteen, Dunfanaghy, third Friday; M. Trimensy.
Donegal, last Wednesday; J. W. M'Dermott.
Dunfanaghy, second Tuesday; D. M'Kelvey.
Dungloe, third Thursday; W. Hanlon.
Glenties, first Monday; D. M'Devitt.
Killybegs, second Monday; J. Crawford.
Letterkenny, second Wednesday; H. E. Peoples.
Malin, first Wednesday; H. W. Hewston.
Milford, second Thursday; B. D. Heuston.
Moville, first Tuesday; John M'Devitt
Newtown Cunningham, first Friday; G. W. Kearns.
Pettigo, last Friday; R. P. Edwards.
Ramelton, second Tuesday; G. Doherty.
Raphoe, second Saturday; James Kerr.
Rathmullen, second Saturday; George M'Gowan.
Stranorlar, second Wednesday; J. Wallwood.
Tamney, second Friday; G. White.

COUNTY GAOL, LIFFORD.

Board of Superintendence, Sir Edmond S. Hayes, bart.; Sir James Stewart, bart.; A. R. Stewart, esq.; Rev. William Knox; William Fenwick, esq.; B. G. Humfrey, esq.; Johnston Mansfield, esq.; James Johnston, esq.; Francis Mansfield, esq.; J. V. Stewart, esq.; Wm. Sinclair, esq.; R. G. Montgomery, esq.

2 K 2

Public Officials of Donegal from Thom's Irish Almanac and Official Directory - 1847

TABLE of PRICES in 1811.	ARMAGH. Returned by George Ensor, Ardress, Feb. 1811.			CAVAN. Returned by Thomas Armstrong, Templeport Aug. 1811.			DONEGAL. Returned by Mr. O'Donnell, Oct. 1811.			Returned by Mr. Nesbitt, Woodhill, June 1811.		
	£.	s.	d.	£.	s.	d.	£.	s.	d.	£.	s.	d.
a Man the year round	7	0	0	6	16	6	9	2	0	8	0	0
b Woman - do. -	2	5	6	2	0	0	4	11	0	n0	0	0
Carpenter per day -	0	3	3	0	1	8 f	0	2	2	0	3	3
Mason - do. -	0	3	3	0	2	2 g	0	2	6	0	3	3
Slater - do. -	0	3	9½	0	2	6 h	0	3	3	0	3	3
Quarry-man do. -	0	1	4	0	1	0 i	0	3	3	0	2	2
Thresher - do. -	0	1	7½	0	1	0 k	0	1	6	0	1	1
Mason per perch -	0	2	6	0	1	6 l	0	1	6	0	5	5
Slater, per square -	0	9	9	0	10	0	0	5	0	0	7	7
Bricklayer, per perch	0	0	0	0	0	0	0	1	6	0	0	0
Car and Horse per day	0	3	4	0	3	4	0	2	6	0	0	0
A saddle horse do. -	0	0	0	0	0	0	0	3	3	0	4	4
A plough - do. -	0	7	7	0	11	4½	0	5	0	0	0	0
Graz a Cow per week	0	2	2	0	2	6	0	2	0	0	1	6
Ditto a Horse do. -	0	4	4	0	6	6	0	12	0	0	5	8
Blacksmith work pr lb.	0	0	6	0	0	10	0	0	7	0	0	8
Ditto - per day -	0	2	0	0	1	0	0	2	6	0	0	0
Price of iron pr stone	0	2	6	0	4	0	0	3	6	0	3	6
c Fencing per perch -	0	1	1	0	1	0	0	0	0	0	1	3
Turf per kish - - -	0	1	0	0	0	6 m	0	2	0	0	1	8
Sea-coal pr bar. Swans.	0	5	0	0	0	0	0	0	0	0	0	0
Kilkenny Coal, cwt.	0	0	0	0	0	0	0	0	0	0	0	0
Culm, per barrel -	0	0	0	0	0	0	0	0	0	0	0	0
Furze, per thousand	0	0	0	0	0	0	0	0	0	0	0	0
Heath per faggot -	0	0	0	0	0	0	0	0	0	0	0	0
Charcoal per barrel, which is necessary to light the Stone Coal - - -	0	0	0	0	0	0	0	0	0	0	0	0
Oak - per foot -	0	5	5	0	5	0	0	4	0	0	3	0
Ash - do - -	0	3	3	0	0	0	0	3	0	0	4	0
Laths, per hundred	0	5	5	1 pr thousd			0	0	0	0	0	0
Bricks, per thousand	2	2	0	0	0	0	1	10	0	1	2	9
Lime, per barrel -	0	2	4	0	1	0	0	1	4	0	1	4
d Plough timber -	0	11	4½	0	8	0	0	0	0	0	0	0
A Car mounted -	6	0	0	4	11	0	6	0	0	2	5	6
Bran, per cwt. -	0	6	6	-	-	-	0	0	0	0	0	0
Potatoes, per stone -	0	0	3½	0	0	4	0	0	4½	0	0	3
Butter, salt, per cwt.	5	0	0	5	5	0	6	0	0	4	0	0
——— fresh, per lb	0	1	0	0	0	10	0	0	11	0	0	10
Hay, per ton - -	4	11	0	2	5	6	3	8	3	2	5	6
Whiskey, per gallon	0	10	10	0	7	0	0	8	6	0	5	0
Ale, per quart - -	0	0	4	0	0	4	0	0	3½	0	0	4

A comparison of Prices in Donegal and other Ulster counties in 1811.

Chapter 12   National School Pupil Registers

The National School system was established in Ireland in 1831 predating the English National Schools. From pre-Norman times education in Ireland had been synonymous with religion, at first Christian and later Catholic. The Reformation and later the Penal laws curtailed this severely. Irish youth sought an education overseas in countries which were both Catholic and pro-Irish. Towards the end of the penal era at the close of the 18th century the 'Hedge school' was favoured by the Catholic clergy as a type of parish school. The State church and civil authority now being Protestant and English saw the need to impose its own system of education on the bulk of the population. Initially it sought a non-denominational model based on Joseph Lancaster's ideas and although this was admirable in concept it proved ineffective in practice.

In 1835 'The Report of the Commission on Public Instruction' was produced and it listed within each parish all the schools at the time; their names; locations; teacher's names; sources of funds; pupil number and sex; subjects being taught; pupil numbers and whether these were increasing or decreasing. The report covered 10,000 schools throughout Ireland.

From 1832-1870, 2,500 National schools were established in Ulster. The Commissioners from the outset kept strict control on what was being taught and they initially produced a series of textbooks for the schools. From 1872 'payment by results' was introduced for the teachers and this effectively meant the pupils being examined in reading, writing, and arithmetic primarily and later in other subjects. The teacher was paid a sum for each subject passed by each pupil and this was added to their basic salary. 'Payment by results' was abolished in 1900 when a new child centred curriculum was introduced. In 1924 the newly created Free State's Department of Education assumed responsibility for the National schools.

In 1924 the newly created Irish Free State 'Department of Education' took control of those schools within its territory.

The Co. Donegal pupil registers can be found either in the schools themselves, in the PRONI or in the National Archives. Over 600 registers were recently deposited at the National Archives and a significant number have

already been listed. The registers for County Donegal date from the second
half of the 19th century.

All the registers contain a pro forma layout and the information contained is:
1. Pupils name and address (townland).
2. Date of entry to school.
3. Religion.
4. Age last birthday or actual date of birth.
5. Father or mother's occupation.
6. Attendances per annum.
7. Subjects studied and examined in (e.g. Reading, Writing,
   Spelling, Grammar, Arithmetic, Geography, Needlework).

The pupil registers available in the National Archives (See address p. 83) are:

Co. Donegal: National School Pupil Registers
(At National Archives)

School	Boys	Girls	Mixed
Ballaghstrang		1871-1906	
Ballystrong	1904-1962	1905-1964	
Ballyratton/Castlecanny	1872-1955		
Ballysaggart		1890-1965	
Barr Na Cuile	1945-1964		
Bredagh Glen	1939-1955		
Carnshanagh		1874-1938	
Carrick Na Horna		1915-1963	
Carrowbeg		1874-1940	
Cashelard	1878-1957	1874-1961	
Cavan Garden	1914-1965	1914-1965	
Corravady	1962-1966	1895-1971	
Derryhenny		1874-1962	
Derry Loughan	1873-1962		
Drumbeg	1915-1966		1904-1966
Glenalla	1872-1960	1881-1953	
Gola Island	1873-1962		
Gulladuff/Moville		1871-1949	
Inishkeragh Island	1886-1953	1929-1954	
Inishmean Island	1886-1957	1886-1957	
Kinelargy Roberston	1885-1943	1898-1942	
Lifford	1876-1946	1874-1945	
Lissinisk/Convoy	1865-1963	1874-1961	
Lough Eske	1857-1956	1867-1951	

School	Boys	Girls	Mixed
Loughmuck	1917-1963	1916-1963	
Meenatole	1866-1963	1892-1963	
Muff	1919-1942	1920-1950	
Naomh Marta Magh Ene		1963-1965	
Narin	1880-1941	1880-1940	
Ray	1899-1965	1887-1965	
Slieve League		1876-1953	
Straleel	1914-1965	1932-1963	
St. Johnston		1950-1974	
Tulloghabegley	1878-1956		
Tullybeg			1880-1957
Tullymore		1913-1945	

Gallagher   *Ó Gallchobhair*

The Gallaghers, who were one of the principal septs of Donegal, are still very numerous there. They claimed absolute seniority over the Cineal Connail, the royal family of Connall Gulban, son of the great 4th-century King Niall of the Nine Hostages.

A translation from the Irish for their name, gallchobhair (foreign help), was possibly acquired in the three centuries when they were marshalls in the armies of the O Donnells.

Their notabilities in the main were clerical. Six O Gallaghers were Bishop of Raphoe in Donegal.

Redmond O Gallagher, Bishop of Derry, helped the Armada sailors wrecked off Donegal and was executed by the English.

Frank Gallagher, a journalist who fought in the civil war, was the first editor of De Valera's newspaper, the *Irish Press*. Patrick Gallagher of Donegal, known as 'Paddy the Cope', initiated the idea of co-operative farming.

Abstract from Ida Grehan's "Pocket Guide to Irish Family Names"
Appletree Press, Belfast 1985.

Chapter 13   Donegal Surnames & Family Histories

By the 10th century Irish surnames, almost all of which derive from forenames, were being used such as O'Neill (O'Neill - 'descendant of Niall') and O'Donnell (O'Domhnaill - descendant of Domhnaill'). The O'Neills and O'Donnells became powerful clans in alliance with other clans, exerting an influence well beyond Tir Connell and Ulster in the early mediaeval period.

An O'Donnell sept was based in Kilmacrenan and were erenaghs in Fahan. The majority of Co. Donegal surnames are Gaelic in origin and some surnames are said to be typical of Co. Donegal e.g. Friel and McGonigle. The following list cites some surnames long associated with Co. Donegal.

Surname		Origin
BARR		From the placename Barr in Ayrshire Came to Donegal after Ulster Plantation
BARRON	Gael MacBarúin	Small landowners from England or Scotland
BONNER		Part of the O'Cráimhsighe sept and noted in Ireland in 1095
BOYLE	Gael O'Baoighill	Irish name since mediaeval period and Scots name since Plantation
BRADLEY	Gael O'Brolacháin	Both indigenous Irish and west of Scotland septs

Surname		Origin
BRESLIN	Gael O'Breasláin	Long associated with lands in Iniskeel parish. Name sometimes anglicised to Brice
CARLIN	Gael O'Cairealláin	Erenaghs in Clonleigh parish
COLL	Gael MacColla	Gallowglass family from Argyllshire who arrived in Ulster in 16th century
CONAGHAN	Gael O'Cinneacháin	Believed to derive from Cunningham
COYLE	Gael MacGiolla Chomhghaill	Lands in Meeragh, Kilmacrenan barony
DIVER	Gael O'Duibhidhir	Sept renowned in medieval Tirconnell
DOHERTY	Gael O'Dochartaigh	Descended from Niall Noigiallach and overlords of Inishowen until 1609
DUFFY	Gael O'Dubhthaigh	Erenaghs of both Templecrone and Culdaff parishes for 800 years
FRIEL	Gael O'Firghil	Descended from Eoghan son of Niall Noigiallach. Erenaghs of Conwal parish
GALLAGHER	Gael O'Gallchobhair	Powerful sept allied to O'Donnells and based in Ballybeit and Ballyneglack
GILLAN	Gael O'Giolláin	Descended from Eoghan son of Niall
GILLESPIE	Gael MacGiolla Easpuig	Erenaghs of Kilrean and Kilcar parish in medieval period
GORMLEY	Gael O'Goirmleadhaigh	Rulers of Raphoe until driven out by O'Donnells in 14th century
GRANT	Norm Fr. 'great'	Norman family who came to Scotland and later Ulster
HARKIN	Gael O'hEarcáin	Erenaghs of Clonca parish, Inishowen

Surname		Origin
HEGARTY	Gael O'hEighceartaigh	Descended from Eoghan son of Niall. Settled in Inishowen
HERRON	Gael O'hEaráin	Probably from Scotland arriving in pre-Plantation times
KERR	Gael MacIlhair - Norse 'Kjarr'	Scots/Irish/Viking origins
LOGUE	Gael O'Maolmhaodhóg	Sept came from Galway to Donegal
MACAULEY	Gael MacAmhlaibh - Norse 'Olafr'	Scots/Irish/Viking origins
MAGEE	Gael Mhaoil Ghaoithe	Erenaghs of Clondahorkey parish
McATEER	Gael Mac an tSaoir	Variant of McIntyre and of Scots/Irish origins
McBRIDE	Gael MacGiollaBhrighde	Erenaghs of Raymunterdoney parish and later of Gweedore
McCAFFERTY	Gael MacEachmharcaigh	Branch of the O'Donnells
McDAID	Gael MacDáighidh	Branch of the O'Dochartaighs
McFADDEN	Gael Pháidin	Scots/Irish origins. Medieval era
McFALL	Gael MacPháil	Ancestral home at Carrickabraghy in Inishowen
McGONIGLE	Gael MacConghail	Erenaghs of Killybegs parish and ecclesiastics in Raphoe
McGOWAN	Gael MacGabhann	Erenaghs of Inishmacsaint parish
McLAUGHLIN	Gael McLochlainn	Erenaghs of Grellagh and Moville parish

Surname		Origin
McNULTY	Gael Mac an Ultaigh	Sept associated with the O'Donnells
MORRISON	Gael Muirgheasáin	Erenaghs of Clonmany parish and holder of St. Colmcille's relic the 'Miosach'
MULLIGAN	Gael O'Maolagáin	Sept and lords or Tir MacCartan in Boylagh and Raphoe baronies
PATTEN	Gael O'Peatáin	Irish sept of Ballybofey and English Pattons of Clondahorkey
QUIGLEY	Gael O'Coigligh	Sept based in Inishowen
SHIELS	Gael O'Siadhail	Sept based in Inishowen descended from Niall Noigiallach
SWEENEY	Gael MacSuibhne	Gallowglass family from Argyll who settled at Fanad
WARD	Gael Mac an Bhaird	Hereditary bards to the O'Donnells, based at Lettermacward

Family Histories

Gaelic society had its 'fili' (learned poets) who would write special tributes to the chieftains and clans. They also could recite from memory long genealogies of these clans and this oral tradition preceded any written genealogies. Monastic scholars later recorded this oral tradition in written form.

Monks based at an abbey near Ballyshannon completed a literary work in 1636 of Gaelic history and genealogy from extant sources of the time. It was known as the 'Annals of the Four Masters' or the 'Annals and History of the Kingdom of Ireland'.

The first genealogies printed in a commercial context appertained to the aristocracy in England and Anglo-Irish families in Ireland. In the Victorian era a series of county histories were produced which included family histories of renowned families including their coats of arms. The Genealogical Office (est. 1552) whose function is still heraldic i.e., granting of coats of arms, did a certain amount of commissioned research into families and thus has a large collection of Irish family histories. It is at present producing a computerised index to these. It also accepted donated family histories.

The practice of publishing family histories by the general public began in the 19th century and these can be found in various repositories. The NLI, the LDS centre at Utah, Society of Genealogists (London), Linen Hall Library (Belfast), and various heritage centres and family history societies all have collections of published and unpublished family histories.

The following list is of Co. Donegal family histories that appear in printed works. Others will also be found within the repositories mentioned in this book.

Family Histories

Alexander	Ahilly	Visitation of Ireland (vol 3) F.A. Crisp (1911)
Crawford	Ballyshannon	Visitation of Ireland (vol 2) F.A. Crisp (1911)
Crawford	Ballyshannon	'Crawford of Donegal and how they came there'. R. Crawford (1886)
Cunningham	Donegal(1100-1800)	Deputy Keeper. PRONI Report. 1951-53 (pp 10-90)
Dever	Ballyshannon	Burkes Colonial Gentry
Dickson & Connolly	Ballyshannon	Donegal Annual 4(1959)
Dills	Fanad	Donegal Annual 34 (1982)
Downey	Donegal	'A History of the Protestant Families of Cos. Sligo, Fermanagh and Donegal. L.C. Downey (1930)
Early	Donegal	'A History of the Family of Early in America; The Ancestors and Descendants of Jeremiah Early who came from Donegal'. S.S. Early 1896
Elder	Donegal	Deputy Keeper.PRONI Report. 1951-53 (pp10-108)
Fitzgerald	Ballyshannon	Kildare Journal III
Harvey	Inishowen	'The Harvey Families of Inishowen' G.H. Harvey (1927)
Hewetson	Ballyshannon	PRSAI/40 (1910)
Kilpatrick	Donegal	DK. PRONI Report. 1951-53(p.10)
Lecky	Donegal	DK/PRONI Report. 1951-53 (p.10)
Marshall	Manorcunningham	G.F. Marshall (1931)
Montgomery	Moville	Visitation of Ireland (vol 2) F.A. Crisp (1911)
O'Cannon	Tirchonaill	Don Ann 12(2) 1978
O'Cleirigh	Tir Conaill	P. Walsh (1938)
Paterson	Plaister & Swillymount	Visitation of Ireland (vol 2) F.A. Crisp (1911)
Pattons & Dills	Springfield	Don Ann 11(1) 1974
White	Lough Esk Castle	Visitation of Ireland (vol 2) F.A. Crisp (1911)

Wrays	Donegal	'Wrays of Donegal' C.V. Trench. C.V. Trench (1945) (-includes history of Wray, Donnelly, Johnston, Waller, MacDaniel, Atkinson & Jackson)
Young	Inishowen	'Three Hundred years in Inishowen' A. Young (1929) (- Pedigree of Young, Hart, Harvey, Doherty, Gage, Knox, Montgomery, Cary, Davenport, Body, Benson, Vaughan, Latham, McLaughlin, Crofton, Hamilton, Skipton, Richardson, Stuart, Day, Stavely, Laurance, Homan, Ffolliott, Cuff, Synge, Nesbitt, Ball, Chichester, Smith, Torrens, Ussher).

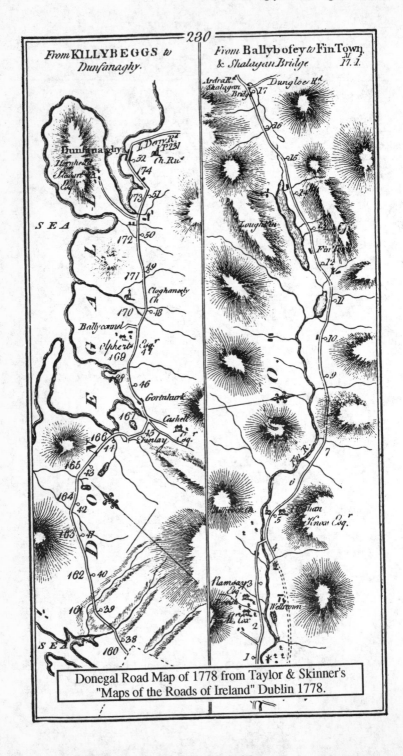

Donegal Road Map of 1778 from Taylor & Skinner's "Maps of the Roads of Ireland" Dublin 1778.

Chapter 14　County Donegal: A Bibliography

The following is a list of books on a wide variety of Donegal places, people and history. They are an historical and genealogical resource for the family historian interested in County Donegal. Not included are articles from journals which are both numerous and interesting and should also be consulted. The major journals publishing articles on Donegal are listed on p.x. A list of journals publishing Donegal material is also provided

Published Works

ALLINGHAM, H. Ballyshannon, Its History and Antiquities, Derry, 1879

AALEN, F.H. & BRODY, H. Gola, The Life and Last Days of an Island Community, 1969. Cork.

BELL, R. The Book of Ulster Surnames, Belfast, 1988.

BONNER, B. Our Inis Eoghain Heritage, Dublin, 1984.

BONNER, B. That Audacious Traitor, Dublin, 1975.

BONNER, B. Where Aileach Guards, Dublin, 1974.

BONNER, B. Redford Glebe; Story of an Ulster Townland, 1978.

BOYD, J.I.C. The Londonderry and Lough Swilly Railway, Truro, 1982.

CAMPBELL, S.M. The Laggan and Its People, 1986.

CARVILLE, G. Assaroe Abbey of the Morning Star, Belfast, 1989.

CONAGHAN, P. Bygones: New Horizons on the History of Killybegs, Killybegs, 1989.

DOHERTY, W.J. Inisowen & Tirconnell, Dublin 1895.

DOLAN, L. Land War And Eviction in Derryveagh 1840-1865, Dundalk, 1980.

FITZGERALD, J. & McCREADIE. Glen War & Oughterlin.

FITZGERALD, J. Holy wells of Inishowen, Carndonagh, 1975.

FITZGERALD, J. Mass Rocks of Inishowen, Carndonagh, 1975.

FOX, R. The Tory Islanders: A People of the Celtic Fringe, Cambridge, 1978.

GWYNN, S. Highways & Byways in Co. Donegal & Antrim, London, 1928.

HARKIN, M & McCARROL, S. Carndonagh, Carndonagh, 1985.

HARKIN, Wm. Scenery & Antiquities of NW Donegal, Derry, 1893.

HARRISON, G. St. Eunan's Cathedral (Raphoe), 1988.

HERITY, M. Glencolmcille, Dublin 1971.

HILL, G. Facts from Gweedore 1845-1847, Dublin 1854. Reprint Belfast 1971.

LACY, B. Archaeological Survey of Co. Donegal, Lifford, 1983.

LUCAS, L. Mevagh Down the Years, Belfast, 1983.

MAGHTOCHAIR. Inishowen, Its History, Traditions & Antiquities, Derry, 1867.

MAGUIRE, V. History of the Diocese of Raphoe, Dublin.

MAGUIRE, W.A. Living Like A Lord 'Marquis of Donegal' 1769-1844, Belfast, 1984.

McCARRON, E. Life in Donegal 1850-1900, Dublin, 1981.

McGILL, L. In Conall's Footsteps, Dingle, 1992.

McGILL, P.J. Parish of Ardara, 1976.

McGILL, P.J. Parish of Killaghte, 1968.

McGLINCHEY, C. The Last of the Name, Belfast, 1986.

MITCHELL, B. Irish Passenger Lists 1847-1871 (ships from Derry), Baltimore, 1988.

MURPHY, D. Derry, Donegal & Modern Ulster 1790-1921, Derry 1982.

O'CARROLL, D. The Guns of Dunree, 1986.

O'GALLACHAIR, P. History of Landlordisim in Donegal, Ballyshannon, 1975.

O'GALLACHAIR, P. Parish of Carn, 1975.

O'GALLACHAIR, P. Finner: Where Erne & Drowes Meet the Sea, 1961.

SHEARMAN, H. Ulster, London, 1949.

SWAN, H.P. The Book of Inishowen Buncrana, 1938.

QUEENS UNIV (pub in progree). Ordnance Survey Memoirs; Co. Donegal, 1834.

YOUNG, A. Three Hundred Years in Inishowen, Belfast, 1929.

Journals

DONEGAL ANNUAL (Journal of the Donegal Historical Society)

DERRIANA (Journal of the Derry Diocesan Historical Society).

CLOGHER RECORD (Journal of the Clogher Diocesan Historical Society).

Chapter 15   Useful Addresses

DONEGAL ANCESTRY LTD
Old Meeting House
Back Lane
Ramelton, Co. Donegal

Their archive includes a substantial amount of Co. Donegal parish registers and other genealogical material.

NATIONAL LIBRARY OF IRELAND
Kildare Street
Dublin 2

Archive includes Catholic parish registers (m/film) up to 1880: Tithes (m/film); Primary Valuation (m/fiche); Irish newspapers and journals; Estate Papers; Trade Directories; Family Histories

NATIONAL ARCHIVES
Bishop Street
Dublin 8

Archive includes 1901 & 1911 Census; pre 1901 Census extracts;Tithes (m/film); Primary Valuation (m/fiche); Pension Claims (1911-1921) Estate Papers; Surviving Wills & Administrations.

GENERAL REGISTER OFFICE
Joyce House
8 Lombard Street
Dublin 2

Civil births, marriages and deaths from 1864 and Church of Ireland marriages from 1845. (research charge)

CHURCH OF JESUS CHRIST OF LATTER DAY SAINTS
Family History Centre
The Willows
Glasnevin
Dublin 11

Holds GRO indexes (m/film) and certificates for various years; miscellaneous genealogical records.

GENEALOGICAL OFFICE
Kildare Street
Dublin 2

Archive includes large collection of family histories. Consultancy service offered for fee.

VALUATION OFFICE OF IRELAND
6 Ely Place
Dublin 1

Holds original Primary Valuation Books; re-valuation books up to 1960's Still operating as Valuation Office.

LAND COMMISSION
Bishop Street
Dublin 8 (restricted access-same building as National Archives)

Useful holdings include details of land sales with landowners and tenant rental lists.

REPRESENTATIVE CHURCH BODY LIBRARY
Braemor Park
Rathgar
Dublin 14

Archive includes substantial Church of Ireland registers (mostly m/films) and odd genealogical material.

O'DOCHARTAIGH RESEARCH CENTRE
Inch Island
Co. Donegal

A user friendly family run genealogical centre specialising in Co.Donegal family records. Research fee.

DONEGAL HISTORICAL SOCIETY
Sec. Kathleen Emmerson
Cluain Barron
Ballyshannon
Co. Donegal

Produces Donegal Annual.

DONEGAL COUNTY LIBRARY
Letterkenny
Co. Donegal

Local history collection, includes 1901 & 1911 Census and other genealogical material.

DONEGAL COUNTY: ARCHIVE CENTRE
The Courthouse, The Diamond
Lifford
Co. Donegal

(see page 86) Holds Poor Law (Workhouse records), Estate records, and other local authority papers. Open only by appointment with Donegal Co. Library (see above)

GENEALOGY CENTRE HERITAGE LIBRARY
14 Bishop Street
Derry
Co. Derry

Co. Derry archive also contains material on Inishowen parishes, Co. Donegal. Research fee.

PUBLIC RECORD OFFICE (NORTHERN IRELAND) Balmoral Avenue Belfast Co. Antrim	Holds genealogical material relating to Co. Donegal
CHURCH OF JESUS CHRIST OF LATTER DAY SAINTS FAMILY HISTORY CENTRE Hollywood Road Belfast Co. Antrim	Offers similar genealogical material as Dublin centre.
PUBLIC RECORD OFFICE Ruskin Avenue Kew Richmond Surrey England	Holds historical and genealogical relating to Ireland

References cited

KINEALY, CHRISTINE, Presbyterian Church Records in **Irish Church Records**. Flyleaf Press, Dublin 1992

RYAN, JAMES G., Catholic Church Records in **Irish Church Records**. Flyleaf Press, Dublin 1992

REFAUSSE, RAYMOND, Church of Ireland Records in **Irish Church Records**. Flyleaf Press, Dublin 1992

KELLY, MARION, The Records of the Methodist Church in Ireland in **Irish Church Records**. Flyleaf Press, Dublin 1992

DONEGAL COUNTY COUNCIL; COUNTY ARCHIVE CENTRE

Liam O Ronain (County Librarian)

Since the early days of the library service in County Donegal, the County Library has been entrusted with the records of public bodies in the County — Boards of Guardians, Rural District Councils etc. In addition a number of MSS and sets of private papers have been given to the Library. For many years these were located in unsuitable accommodation, in the basement of Lifford Courthouse. In 1985 the County Council secured funding from the Special Border Areas Programme of the European Regional Development Fund to renovate Lifford Courthouse, and since 1986 the County Archive Centre has been located in purpose-designed accommodation in the Courthouse.

Lifford Courthouse is the oldest public building in the province of Ulster still in use. The renovation provided, in addition to the County Archive Centre, a Community Library, an exhibition centre and a multi-use space, intended for Council receptions, recitals, readings etc.

The County Archive Centre is a large well-lit space on the first floor of the Courthouse with access by a spiral staircase from the Community Library, and access to a wing of the Courthouse, presently occupied by Circuit Court staff, which may be available in the future to accommodate stack shelving for the Archive Centre. The archive material is stored on specially designed wooden shelving. There is space for about ten researchers.

Boards of Guardians

There were 8 Boards of Guardians in Donegal, covering the Poor Law Unions of Ballyshannon, Donegal, Dunfanaghy, Glenties, Inishowen, Letterkenny, Milford and Stranorlar. Parts of the east of the County were included in Derry and Strabane Unions, but their records are not held in Lifford. The Minute Books of the Boards run to over 100 ft. and they date from the 1840's to 1923. As well as the Minute Books the following may be of use in genealogical research:

Punishment Book 1879 – c. 1900: 165 entries giving name, offence and punishment: no details of location.

Separate register (September 1913 – March 1922) giving full name, address, age, occupation and religion for individuals admitted to or discharged from the Fever Hospital or Infirmary of Glenties Poor Law Union.

Outdoor Relief, Admission and Discharge Book (1908 – 11), probably Inishowen PLU, including name of person, or head of family relieved and amount of relief allowed.

Workhouse Admission Register, December 1850 – October 1866) Glenties PLU: 4,960 names giving age, occupation, religion, location, date of admission and discharge.

Indoor Relief Register (1856 – 1915) probably for Dunfanaghy PLU: 5,000 names with age, address, religion, occupation and date of discharge or death.

Milford Workhouse Indoor Register (1880 – 97) (BG119/G/3): 5,000 names.

Donegal Union Indoor Admission and Discharge Book (1919 – 21).

Ballyshannon Clothing Receipt Book (April 1905 – September 1924).

Glenties Indoor Relief Register (1914 – 1921).

Inishowen Workhouse Admission Register (September 1849 – May 1859) (BG97/G/2): 5,000 names. At the back of the book there are lists of orphans and deserted children hired out of the Workhouse (May 1853 and 1 January 1857 – 1 January 1858), noting name, person to whom hired and employment (mainly herding cattle).

Indoor Relief Register (March 1914 – September 1924) possibly for Donegal PLU.

Dispensary Committee Minute Book (March 1852 – 1899) Stranorlar PLU.

Report Book of Visiting Committee of Milford Union Workhouse (6 April 1846 – 25 May 1912).

Minute Book of Co. Donegal Branch of Irish Medical Association 1903 – 1977.

Grand Jury Public Orders (1831) with manuscript annotations.

Letterkenny Workhouse Admission Register (1864 – 77) (BG109/E/1): 4,120 names.

Workhouse Admission Register (1907 – 11) Inishowen (?) Workhouse (BG97/G/6): 5,000 names.

Indoor Relief Register (1907) Glenties: 5,140 names.

Indoor Relief Register (1899 – 1907) Inishowen (BG97/G/5): 5,000 names.

Abstract from 'North Irish Roots' Vol.2 (5), 1990

Index